Elite Marketing Machine

How to Create An Avalanche of Local Customers

Jason Laird, B.A., M.S.O.M, L.Ac.

Chief Strategist

www.EliteMarketingMachine.com

www.EliteMarketingMachine.com
quote@EliteMarketingMachine.com

ISBN-10:1511661968

ISBN-13: 978-1511661966

This publication is designed to provide general information regarding the subject matter covered. However, laws and practices often vary from state to state and country to country are subject to change. Because each factual situation is different, specific advice should be tailored to the particular circumstances. For this reason, the reader is advised to consult with an advisor regarding that individual's specific situation.

The author has taken reasonable precautions in the preparation of this book and believes that the facts as presented in this work are accurate as of the date written. However, neither the author nor the publisher assumes any responsibility for any errors or omissions. The author specifically disclaims any liability resulting from the use or application of the information contained in this book, and the information is not intended to serve as legal advice related to individual situations.

Table of Contents

For Amber, Sterling, Rogan, Judi and Damon

About The Author

Jason Laird, MSOM, L.Ac. has owned and operated several successful businesses over the last decade. Creighton University 1993

An injury during Marine Corps Officer Candidate School at the age of 27 prevented him from entering the Jet Flight Training Program.

He instead went on to create custom artwork and photography for Celebrities including Craig T. Nelson, Jason Priestley, Nigel Olsson (Drummer for Elton John), Race Car driver Kyle Petty, Baseball player Mike Devereaux and Quarterback John Elway to name a few.

Jason then received a Masters Degree in Acupuncture and Chinese Herbology from the Academy of Oriental Medicine at Austin - AOMA. He moved back to his home State of Wyoming and created one of the most successful Acupuncture practices in the world.

He also created a topical herbal Pain Relief formula for his mother Judi because she had debilitating Arthritis in her hands. It was so painful that she couldn't button her blouse or hold on to a glass of water. Because he made it out of love for his mother, he made it to work. Pain Relief Miracle has since been sold in over 22 countries and online at www.PainReliefMiracle.com.

Jason and his wife Amber raise 4 children and operate The Sterling Hotel in Casper, WY. They are also active Real Estate investors and split their time between Casper, Wyoming and Austin, Texas.

A prolific entrepreneur, he studies Marketing extensively and has mentorships with some of the most brilliant and successful Internet Marketers in the world. Jason uses his knowledge to successfully promote his own businesses both on and offline.

Jason founded EliteMarketingMachine.com to assist other Local Professionals and Business owners to create more revenue and freedom, grow their business and dominate their market.

Curse of the Golden Handcuffs

In an effort to become a professional in our chosen field, we have unwittingly become indentured servants to ourselves and our debts and quite willingly and without contemplating the consequences, bound our hands behind our backs with shiny Golden Handcuffs.

Our practice and/or business provides a living and a lifestyle envious to most of the modern world and yet robs us of the most basic freedoms of life. We cannot just leave at a moments notice or turn our practice over to a "temp." No one can perform the procedures, the treatments or the one-on-one sessions we provide our clients or patients.

When you take a vacation, usually all income ceases for the time you are out of the office and your 2 week vacation really is... too weak. Many times you don't even begin to relax until just before having to get on the plane to go back home. And all the while, you have been worrying about everything you "should have done" or have to do upon your return, causing you to not really be present for your family.

Because I have been there, I know the unique struggles a successful practice brings, I discovered the solution for myself that keeps the income flowing even while I sleep. The systems I have put into place for myself and my family are now available to my Consulting Clients.

If a client qualifies, we help you achieve **Total Market Domination** in your chosen city and elevate your status to that of an Industry Expert. Causing you to be the obvious choice for service to your customers.

Although we provide many top level design and marketing services for the general public, Our Web Domination Package is by application only and we only accept ONE Client in each field in any given city. i.e. One Personal Injury Attorney, One Dentist, One Chiropractor etc.

This allows us to work only with serious clients and implement our unique systems into your business which will cause **money to rain from the sky into your wallet! Call Us Today for The Golden Key!**

Will That Key Be For You?

Or Your Competition?

Secret Formula used by the Rich and Famous to build their fortunes

We've all heard from Psychology, we have 2 parts to our mind. The conscious and the sub-conscious. Here's how use both to get what you want in life!

When you plant the seed of what you want in your mind, your mind makes your body change its vibration and everything you want is attracted to you through the "Law of Attraction!"

This formula was first written about in 1937 by Napoleon Hill in his book "Think and Grow Rich". I have outlined the basic formula that he describes. For a more detailed description, buy that book.

If you could create your ideal "dream" life, no matter how far out or "impossible" you or someone else may think it is, what would it look like? What would you own, what would you drive, what does your house look like? Where in the world do you live etc?

No matter how crazy they sound, write them down in a bulleted list. If you want a $548,000 Yellow and Black Lamborghini Aventador or a $25 Million Dollar House on the beach, write it down. Maybe you want to be a famous singer or an actor on Broadway, write it down.

Whatever you want, write it down! No one needs to see this but you. And it's actually preferable that you don't show it to anyone so they don't interject their skepticism and lack of dreamability.

Pretend you are a child again and use your innate gift of imagination. Look around you... EVERYTHING you see, everything we use, every gadget, tool or even the piece of furniture you are sitting on, was first an idea in someone's mind.

On the top of the page write the date you want your goals to materialize into your life.

Don't set the date too close but don't put it 15 years into the future either. It could be 6 months or a year.

Write down 20 or so things you want in your life. Write them in the present tense as if you already have them.

For example:
I own a 2014 Yellow and Black Lamborghini Aventador LP 720-4 Roadster 50 Anniversario 2dr Convertible

I own a $4.7 Million 5 Bedroom home with beautiful panoramic views of Okanagan Lake in British Columbia. It has a 3 car heated garage, a heated pool and hot tub etc. Google "Nautical Vista" for ideas.

I am a highly sought after and respected Consultant in my field

Here is the "Secret Ingredient"...

Every day, maybe 2 or even 3 times a day, re-write your perfect life over and over again. The more impressions you make on your sub-conscious mind, the quicker the results will materialize for you.

Summary of "The Science of Getting Rich"
by Wallace D. Wattles

Get a Free pdf copy of this classic book here:
www.EliteMarketingMachine/SOGR

There is a thinking stuff from which all things are made, and which, in its original state, permeates, penetrates, and fills the interspaces of the universe.

A thought in this substance produces the thing that is imaged by the thought.

Man can form things in his thought, and by impressing his thought upon formless substance can cause the thing he thinks about to be created.

In order to do this, man must pass from the competitive to the creative mind; otherwise he cannot be in harmony with the Formless Intelligence, which is always creative and never competitive in spirit.

Man may come into full harmony with the Formless Substance by entertaining a lively and sincere gratitude for the blessings it bestows upon him. Gratitude unifies the mind of man with the intelligence of Substance, so that man's thoughts are received by the Formless.

Man can remain upon the creative plane only by uniting himself with the Formless Intelligence through a deep and continuous feeling of gratitude .

Man must form a clear and definite mental image of the things he wishes to have, to do, or to become; and he must hold this mental image in his thoughts, while being deeply grateful to the Supreme that all his desires are granted to him.

The man who wishes to get rich must spend his leisure hours in contemplating his Vision, and in earnest thanksgiving that the reality is being given to him.

Too much stress cannot be laid on the importance of frequent contemplation of the mental image, coupled with unwavering faith and devout gratitude. This is the process by which the impression is given to the Formless, and the creative forces set in motion.

The creative energy works through the established channels of natural growth, and of the industrial and social order. All that is included in his mental image will surely be brought to the man who follows the instructions given above, and whose faith does not waver. What he wants will come to him through the ways of established trade and commerce.

In order to receive his own when it shall come to him, man must be active; and this activity can only consist in more than filling his present place. He must keep in mind the Purpose to get rich through the realization of his mental image.

And he must do, every day, all that can be done that day, taking care to do each act in a successful manner. He must give to every man a use value in excess of the cash value he receives, so that each transaction makes for more life; and he must so hold the Advancing Thought that the impression of increase will be communicated to all with whom he comes in contact.

The men and women who practice the foregoing instructions will certainly get rich; and the riches they receive will be in exact proportion to the definiteness of their vision, the fixity of their purpose, the steadiness of their faith, and the depth of their gratitude.

To your success!

Jason

Pro-Level Consultation with Extensive Market Research and Competition Analysis

<u>Any of the Services</u> discussed in this book can be **Done-For-You...**
Fill out the form at <u>www.EliteMarketingMachine.com</u>

For a limited time, we are offering our *Pro-Level Consultation* for **FREE to <u>qualified</u> readers of this book.**

We typically charge $1,000 per Consultation and Implementation Session due to of the extensive research and analysis that my team performs.

You will not find this for free with any other company.

If you want to **compete in the Online or Offline Marketing world,** then you need serious intelligence and a Top Level Consultant.

Take advantage of this offer now and get educated about your current presence online and what your competition is doing!

We need to understand your business, your products and services, your marketing goals, as well as your past and present marketing efforts to help us devise a sound marketing strategy for you.

Your Free Consultation includes the following:

- Keyword Research
- Competition Analysis
- Website Structure Analysis
- Online Presence Report

Keyword Research

We identify and recommend keywords and keyword phrases for you based on your business, products or services, and the types of searcher-intent you want to target. You will gain knowledge about the keywords your potential customers are actually typing in when they are searching for the products or services that you're offering.

You will see keywords and keyword phrases relevant to your business with the corresponding search volume, relative SEO and PPC competition, as well as the average cost per click to get an idea of the pay per click advertising value of these terms.

Competition Analysis Report

In this report, you will see how your competitors are ranking for the keywords and keyword phrases we have covered in the Keyword Research Report.

Armed with this knowledge, you can decide what keywords you want to compete for intensively. At the same time, you can choose strong, relevant keywords with relatively low to medium competition, or keywords that are apparently ignored by your competition. This can help you easily rank in Google's search results.

Website Structure Analysis Report

We will analyze your website's structure and basic attributes to give you an idea of the basic improvements that must be done to begin optimizing your website.

We will analyze your home page for the basic elements that should be present in the right form and in the right quantity, as well as your website's compliance with industry standards. We will also analyze your basic off-site SEO and Social Media presence.

Online Presence Report

We'll show you the major business listings you are showing up in against your competitors. You will see if you are listed in local directories, plus, you will see your citations or the lack of it side-by-side with that of your competition. You will also see an overview of your reputation and reviews compared with that of your competitors.

In order to compete in the online Marketplace, you'll need professional consulting and in-depth research. Lucky for you, we are offering this right now for free to qualified readers of this book.

Visit www.EliteMarketingMachine.com to see if you qualify.

Sincerely,

Jason Laird
Chief Strategist

What To Do Right Now:

Go to www.EliteMarketingMachine.com right now and fill out the form to get started.

Why It's Getting Harder To Get New Customers

Local Businesses are seeing more competition for customers, clients, and patients than ever before.   A recent Small Business Administration study reports that Local Businesses are seeing the largest increase in years.

Since 1990, large corporations have eliminated 4 million jobs and Local Businesses have added 8 million new jobs.

The number of Local Businesses have increased 49% since 1982... that is nearly 12 million new businesses that are all competing for customers.

But it Gets Worse!

Recent statistics show that even after coming out of the hard economic times of the past several years, many Local Businesses are struggling to survive and many will go out of business in the next 3-5 years.

To make matters worse, recent statistics show that most Local Businesses rely on traditional methods of getting clients and those methods have stopped working...

Good News!

There Are Still Plenty of Customers Out There!

It's true and I can tell you that if you are ready to take your business to the next level, the information I am about to share could be worth a fortune to you!

The good news is that it is very likely that you will be able to implement these strategies without having to spend any more than you already are on advertising.

(Don't worry if you aren't spending any money on advertising. I will show you low-cost, effective ways to get your message in front of people that are hungry for your product or service.)

New Customer Getting Methods

So how do you get more customers? Of course there is traditional advertising, cold calling, networking etc. But these are the things that most businesses have been doing from the start and so has the competition.

We need to breathe some fresh air into this area of your business. There are actually 34 methods that can be leveraged to get more clients, but that would probably overwhelm most business owners and I want to give you a few of the most effective ways so you can start and get some success under your belt.

The Initial List We Use With Our Consulting Clients:

- Search Engine Optimization
- Google Adwords
- Social Media Marketing
- Facebook and Adwords Retargeting Pixels
- Online Directories
- Mobile Marketing
- YouTube Marketing
- LinkedIn
- Direct Response Marketing
- Power Referrals
- Trade Publications
- Mobile Marketing
- Trade Show Marketing
- Direct Mail

Let's look at a few that you can implement and get some quick momentum, no matter what type of business you have.

It doesn't matter if you are selling a physical product, a service or an information product, the methods I am about to share will work for you!

Spreading the Word About Your Business!

If you look at traditional advertising like Yellow Pages, the newspaper or TV commercials, these platforms all have one thing in common. They are expensive and there is no real way to measure their effectiveness.

Let's look first at the Yellow Pages... let me ask you a question...
Do you know where your yellow pages book is right now? My guess is that you don't, as a matter of fact you may not even have one in your own home or office. When was the last time you looked in the yellow pages for a business? If you are like me, it was several years ago.

Even though most people don't use them anymore, many businesses still spend thousands of dollars each year on yellow page ads. Studies show that average age of a person who uses yellow pages is over 70 years old. So if this is not your target market, then your marketing dollars may be more effective with modern methods.

I look at TV commercials and Newspaper ads as a place where you spend money telling people all about your product or service and hope they either need it at the exact moment they see the advertisement or remember your ad when they do need your service.

This is "Hope Marketing"

Paying for advertising and hoping you get customers.

Here is a question about the Newspaper...
Do YOU get the local paper on a daily basis?

My guess is probably not, and it is a safe guess because 24 of the top 25 newspapers in the U.S. have seen record declines in sales.

I would also venture to guess that if you do place ads in the newspaper, you can't tell me where I should look to find information about YOUR business... that's because even though ads pay for the lions share of the newspaper's publishing costs... they get placed wherever there is space left after the articles are all laid out for maximum readership.

When it comes to TV Commercials, not only is it almost impossible to measure effectiveness, most people watch recorded shows these days and skip the commercials all together. So what is a business owner to do?

DO NOT spend even $1.00 that doesn't bring back $1.00 to $100 quickly and directly.

DO NOT listen to advertising reps that try to convince you your ad will be seen by X amount of people and have no accountability to give you actual SALES RESULTS! *It does you NO GOOD for your ad to be seen by people that don't want or need what you are offering.*

DO: Spend $1.00 on marketing and get back $1.00 to $100 that you can attribute to that $1.00 you spent. Be able to track it.

How the Internet Became Local

Businesses of all types are starting to become aware of what a small percentage of early adopters already know: Internet and Mobile Device platforms have revolutionized marketing.

Thanks to high-speed wireless networks, mobile devices, communications software, and social platforms, marketing has been transformed into a largely digital discipline for Local Businesses.

This media is quickly replacing old school advertising methods such as newspaper ads, printed business directories like the Yellow Pages, direct mail coupons—even radio and TV ads.

Online marketing is also effective whether or not a business currently sells products or services over the Internet. "Brick and Mortar" businesses of all kinds are using these new strategies with impressive results.

Local consumers' increasing usage of the Internet and mobile media are driving businesses to learn how to take advantage of these new platforms so their prospects and customers can find them, hear about them and, ultimately, buy from them.

This is also important because the Internet is interactive. Consumers are sharing their experiences about Local Businesses... Both positive and negative! Not only is it very important for business owners to control the message that they are putting out, but they must also keep track of what people are saying about their business.

Take a look at the statistics: Google has over 3.5 billion searches every day; out of those 105 billion monthly searches, over 28 Billion (or in 27% of all searches) are local. What that means is people are actually putting in a geographic identifier in the search bar.

For instance if you're in Denver and you're looking for a Dentist, chances are you don't just put in "Dentist"; chances are you put in "Denver Dentist" or "Denver Dental office." You type something that identifies where you are geographically.

From there the search engine knows to go find the information that is most relevant for you. After all, if you have a toothache, you don't really care about how great the Dentist in Dallas is if you live in Denver.

The same thing goes for a pizza joint. If you're looking for pizza, you probably aren't just looking for pizza in general; you're looking for it based on where you are located. Here's another amazing statistic: **82% of local searches are followed by an action.** A store visit, a call, an email or a *purchase*! So when people are searching locally, it means they are ready to take an action and more likely to buy. They are a purchase driven consumer!

What is "Mobilegeddon" and Google's Mobile Friendly Update?

On April 21, 2015, Google released a significant new mobile-friendly ranking algorithm that is designed to favor mobile-friendly pages in Google's mobile search results.

The change is so significant that the date was called **Mobilegeddon.**

Check your web site for mobile compatibility on google's Mobile-Friendly Test tool.

https://www.google.com/webmasters/tools/mobile-friendly/

Google's algorithms, which use more than 200 signals that help the search engine predict what a user wants, have been the source of many sleepless nights for many businesses

Google controls two-thirds of the U.S. search market. Algorithm updates with names like Panda and Penguin have caused many Web-based businesses to see their traffic plummet overnight, and profits evaporate.

Google Rolled out Panda in 2011. It ranks sites based on quality and relevance, while Penguin was launched the next year to weed out pages that abuse the use of links to artificially boost traffic.

Mobilegeddon was the biggest algorithm update so far because it focuses on rankings of mobile sites.

This update favors sites that are "mobile-friendly." This means that people who use Google to search for a business on their smartphone may not find many of their favorite sites at the top of the rankings.

Sites that haven't updated could find themselves ranked much lower, which in turn could mean a huge loss of business.

Google has an estimated 65% market share of U.S. Internet searches, wants sites to load quickly and be easy to navigate on a mobile phone.

Google is doing this because it wants consumers to "find content that is not only relevant and timely, but also easy to read and interact with on smaller mobile screens," Google said in a statement.

It's not too late but if your website isn't mobile friendly, get one ASAP. Don't lose customers to your competition.

Capitalizing On Local Searches

The great news is there are a number of ways that we can put information online for people to find when they are searching locally and gain Market Share for your business.

Local Internet Marketing is based on helping Local Business owners put information online where people can find it at the exact time that they are looking for it. That's very important and it's very different than other forms of advertising.

For instance, look at the yellow pages. Stop and ask yourself this question: do you know where your phone book is right now? Probably not... If you're like 80% of the population, you don't have a clue where that giant book is.

The average age of a Yellow Pages user is over 70 years of age!

This means if a business is in the yellow pages alone, they are missing out on the vast majority of their target market.

Remember the Internet uses a technological way of finding the most relevant information about businesses, and nearly everyone uses it. *Old school methods just don't produce enough results to even pay for themselves anymore.*

Alternatively, local Internet Marketing provides a strategy for Local Businesses to put their information in hundreds of different places so that people can find the information at exact time that they need the product or service.

Both in theory and in practice, this has proven to be a much better solution and makes it much easier for the business owner to see the value of their advertising funds rather than just continuing to spend thousands of dollars on ineffective means of marketing.

Pre-Selling Your Business To Customers

Pre-selling your business online is important; in order to make it work, you'll need a great website. In fact, a robust site can actually be the key to the beginning of your Internet Marketing campaign. When you begin looking at the task of promotion, it helps to understand what is involved in the process. You want to generate highly targeted, qualified customers. To do this, you'll need a great-looking, functional website that will garner traffic.

There are several aspects that make up a successful Internet Marketing plan. They should be the building blocks of your campaign. You need to generate interest. Knowing what your target audience wants is the key to giving them content that will be of interest to them.

Since you are marketing via the Internet, you'll be selling the idea of your business to visitors who are seeking the type of information you have to offer. This can serve you well because it takes the guesswork out of figuring out what they need to know. You'll need to include this information on your website. It should be informative and easy to read.

Educate your visitors. Give them something they can use. Instead of just recycling the same information found on other similar websites, make yours unique. Tell your visitors something that will be relevant and important. This is what will keep them coming back time after time.

Create desire. A well built website should give them the desire to want to know more. Keep the content interesting and fresh. Include any new information relevant to the topics pertaining to services offered by your business, or practice.

When you presell your business online, you are preparing your prospects for what is offered in your business. Email marketing is also a great way to get prospects to your site. While the website itself is the starting point for your Internet Marketing plan, the emails you send will be used to entice people into becoming visitors.

Know your market. When you understand who you are talking to, knowing what to tell them will be easier. Your website should be based on your target market. Consider who will likely visit your website. Ask yourself what they will want to know.

Use examples or scenarios on your website. This gives your readers something to relate to in a very direct way. If what you wrote describes that person, you have just come that much closer to gaining a customer. This allows you to create the needed interest that will draw your prospect closer. Include different scenarios. Not all your prospects will be in the same situation. In fact, some may be very different. You can appeal to a wider range of clients by including a number of scenarios.

Make sure the information on your site is clear. Your readers should have no problem understanding your information. Use language that makes sense to the masses. If you must use industry jargon, be sure to explain it. Only use industry language when necessary. Otherwise, explain things in terms that are easy to comprehend. You want your customers to relate to you on a very personal level. This is what will cause a peak in their interest and keep them coming back.

Converting Website Visitors Into Buyers

The key to a successful website is conversion. You ultimately want those who visit your website to become customers/clients/patients. You will need a plan of action in order to make this happen. This plan will enable you to build relationships and create the trust necessary to increase the number of visitors you receive, but to also make them stay. Below are tips that will show you how to implement a site designed with conversion in mind.

Provide quality content about the products and services offered at your business. Make sure it is clear and concise. Information that is easy to understand will appeal to visitors, especially those who are conducting an initial search. Grab your visitor's attention immediately. This means putting the most important information first. Think of the main points you want them to be aware of and make sure these are incorporated before everything else.

Create a website that is easy to navigate. Confusing layouts or content that is difficult to follow will prompt visitors to go elsewhere for information. Write all content with your potential clients in mind. Explain what you can do for them and how helpful your services will be. List the benefits of your services and tell them why they should choose your business.

Design your website specific for the target audience. This means creating each page with respective types of visitors in mind. For example, you might link a specific page to a particular ad. That page might contain information about the services you offer. So, if a visitor is searching specifically for this type of information, it needs to be easily accessible so clients can reach it quickly. This will take the guesswork out of navigating the entire site just to find the information they want.

On the other hand, another visitor might be reading an article about the benefits of your products and services and see a direct link to your home page.

That person isn't necessarily looking for a specific type of information, but rather is searching for something more general. It's all about directing visitors to the right site, and you can use your various advertising mediums to target specific pages.

Implement active thinking… Use an active voice in all your content to keep your visitors motivated. Your copy should be engaging and make them want to continue reading. This is a more dynamic approach and often makes people feel as if they are being spoken to directly. It helps establish a rapport, which can quickly lead to a conversion.

Increase the trust between you and your visitors. Trust is the basis of any good relationship, and when it comes to promoting your business, it will serve you well. You want your prospects to believe in you and feel confident about your product and/or the services you provide.

An effective website begins with a successful online marketing plan. Your business will greatly benefit from well-thought out pages designed specifically with your target market in mind. Use the tips above to build a website that will help your business grow.

Top Five Benefits Of A Great Website

A great website is the most important online marketing tool you can have for your business. It's where much of the relevant information will be located and is your direct link to potential prospects. There are several benefits to having a well-developed site. Below are five of the most important advantages and why they are relevant:

Benefit 1

A great website is essential, it has become a requirement of sorts. Customers expect and look for it. They want to know there is a specific place they can go to get information.

If you fail to establish an Internet presence, your competition will beat you in the online marketing department. Your site can make you stand out from the rest. It should depict who your business is. Tell readers about the services you offer and how they can contact you. Your website should be informative and easy to read and navigate.

Benefit 2

A great website helps build trust. It shows your visitors you have something important to offer and gives them a place to go where they can learn more. Here is where you will have the chance to build your online image. It also shows your expertise in the field.

Benefit 3

A great website increases the odds of others learning about your business. Most people turning to the Internet to obtain information, it is being relied upon to produce results. These results are produced by search engines.

The ultimate goal is to receive high rankings for all your pages. The higher rank of your site, the more visible you'll be online. For this, search engine optimization (SEO) is key. The content of your website should incorporate keywords potential clients will use to find you. A well optimized site will place you high in the rankings.

Benefit 4

Design your site carefully. While you definitely want to keep the content easy to read and navigate, all your pages should be eye-catching.

Choose a theme or look that is relevant to what you are offering. Consider usability while making sure the content and all elements will grab the attention of visitors. A well-designed site that is easy to navigate and contains useful information will prompt them to stay.

Benefit 5

A great website will give a great first impression. This is very important, especially to those who are hearing of you for the first time online. You need pages that look professional, are user-friendly, and will provide your potential customers with everything they'll need to begin taking advantage of your services.

Always include up-to-date information. This is absolutely essential. A site that hasn't been updated in a while will detract from your credibility in the eyes of visitors. You want it to look like there's been activity and you want that activity to be real. Add some useful articles or blog posts. This will show that you visit the site frequently and are in touch with the needs of your customers.

Make sure all contact information is correct. Visitors who are unable to make contact with questions will often go elsewhere. You can avoid this by providing several ways in which they may get in touch. Your website will serve you well if it receives the right attention. Think of it as a part of your overall business and allow it to grow with you.

The Automated Sales Funnel

If Your website is designed properly, it can also serve as an automated "Sales Funnel".

Most people don't respond well to a forceful or "in your face" sales approach anymore. That's why Sales Funnels are so important. They lead prospects through a series of subtle (and welcomed) steps that ultimately result in the desire to buy from you.

This Marketing Strategy should be used by every business to get leads and convert them into customers.

We help our Consulting clients with Sales Funnels that help develop traffic, leads, and sales.

Our Templates include the Free Book Funnel, the Splinter Offer Funnel, The Flash Sale Funnel, Perpetual and Paid Webinar Funnel, The Football Phone Funnel, The Velvet Rope Funnel, The Blog Launch Funnel, The Simple Survey Funnel, Live Event Funnel, Mini Class Launch and more.

These funnels have been tested, extensively, to save time, money, and energy, while increasing revenue.

The 4 Major Rules For Selling

The only purpose of any advertisement, sales letter, or marketing piece is too sell your prospect or customer on taking the action you want them to take.

For a lead generation ad, letter, or e-mail, it might be to have them request more information. For a sales letter, it could be to pick up the phone or go to your website and order.

For a follow-up offer, it could be to upgrade to a more expensive item, buy a second item, or join a Platinum Membership Club for goods or services to be billed monthly to their credit card.

These are just a few examples of the actions you might want your leads or customers to make. But what is consistent is that you are guiding them to take a very specific action.

Your success at accomplishing this will be much greater, and easier when you understand the Four Major Rules of Selling. These Rules apply to anything you write or create. They are the underlying foundation to massive sales success.

Major Selling Rule #1

You must have a quality product.

If your product isn't high quality, you'll have a high rate of returns.

Second, an inferior product kills repeat sales and referrals to other customers. Repeat sales are the true success of any business. It is much more cost effective with a much greater ROI to have customers that already know-like-and trust you. Referrals are extremely profitable because there are usually no marketing costs to make these sales.

Major Selling Rule #2

Create your "Ideal Customer Profile."

This is *extremely* important and you must understand it or you will compromise your sales and profits. When it comes to customers, it is essential to understand that there may be a wide range of customers you might appeal to. But the customer group your business will profit from the most from is your "Ideal Customer."

What Is An "Ideal Customer?"

1. A customer who wants your product or service.
2. A customer who has the ability to pay for your product or service.
3. A customer who has the authority to purchase your product or service.

It seems like these characteristics are obvious, but my experience with thousands of business owners proves this isn't the case. Let's look at each characteristic closely.

1. A Customer Who Wants Your Product Or Service

Seems logical, doesn't it? But not so fast! This can be extremely dangerous. Typically, the most danger occurs when you have a product that proverbially, "everyone needs."

Trying to market to everyone under the sun can be extremely costly and almost always leads to failure. What you really need is a carefully defined type of customer who have specific hot buttons you can appeal to.

The tighter the definition of your market, the easier it is to market to them. For example, people who "Need an Accountant" could be very difficult to market to because there are a wide variety of services to offer and an even wider variety of needs these customers might have.

But if you narrow this group down to people who are having problems with the IRS and are behind with or haven't filed quarterly payments, you now have a tightly defined target market. Creating powerful selling copy aimed at this specific market segment is much easier than dealing with everyone who needs the services of an Accountant.

2. Customers That Can Afford Your Product Or Service.

This is a little subtler and comes in two forms. The first is trying to sell to people who can't afford your product.

The thinking by the business owner seems to go like this: "The person needs what I have to offer it so much that they will find some way to buy even if they can't afford it. Sorry, but that rarely happens.

The second variation is selecting a cash-poor market as your target market and then lowering your prices to try to sell to this market. Another critical error.

You won't have a solid business by selling low cost products to prospects that don't have the financial resources to pay your price.

Businesses choose start up businesses, mom and pop type businesses, college students, or worse as their target market.

This is business and financial suicide. What you really want is a market that has a true need and is willing and able to pay to satisfy that need.

3. A Customer With Authority To Purchase.

This usually happens when an employee of a company responds to your advertisement, mailing, or website.

The employee may have a burning desire to buy your product. But their boss doesn't share their interest and won't authorize the purchase. So, no sale for you.

Creating Your Ideal Customer Profile

Your profits depend on accurately identifying a group of customers who want, can afford, and have the authority to purchase your products or services. And the best way to do that is to create a profile of exactly what that group would look like.

For our example, we'll say you're a Dentist and want to sell Teeth Whitening services. Who would be most likely to buy your products and services?

Obviously, anyone with the majority of their teeth would be a potential customer, but that's too broad of a market.

For one thing, your strongest target market would be people that have stained teeth or at least think they do.

This would eliminate people that already have pearly white teeth that you'd reach by advertising to the masses.

A Sample Ideal Customer would look something like this:

1. Female between the ages of 30-50 within 50 miles of your office.
2. Married with children.
3. Middle to upper income.
4. Subscribes to one or more beauty magazines.
5. Has stained teeth (or wants them whiter than she has currently)
6. Has purchased other teeth whitening related products through the same marketing method you use to sell your products.

That would be a good starting Ideal Customer Profile. After you've tested the market for a while, you may discover certain segments of the group or a different group all together greatly outperform others. You would then give this segment higher priority, and they might eventually become your Ideal Customer Profile. It might prove to be so lucrative to only market to this group that any other efforts would be a waste.

For example, you might discover that 80% of all buyers are Single women who drink red wine 2-3 times a week and coffee every morning in order to be able to wake up to go to work.

And, if you also discovered the amount this group spends is nearly twice as much as other customer groups, you'd be wise to focus all your efforts on these women.

You would focus all of your marketing to appeal to the hot buttons that motivate these ladies to buy.

- Increased Self Confidence
- Healthier Appearance
- Stand out in a crowd
- Higher pay or more responsibility in their job
- Quicker career advancement
- Attract a mate

This was a quick example in creating an Ideal Customer Profile. You should now be able to create one of your own.

One that you can take all the way to the bank!

Major Selling Rule #3

Your Credibility Produces Maximum Profits.

The key to creating an ongoing source of consistently high sales is having credibility in your marketplace.

Businesses that only have 2,000 to 3,000 customers can make small fortunes year after year because they have built flawless credibility with their customers.

A profit of $300 per year per customer comes to $600,000 from a customer base of 2,000. And $900,000 on a customer base of 3,000.

A high degree of credibility with your existing customer base is worth far more than anything else you could possibly imagine.

Many business owners are only focused on the customer at the time of purchase and neglect them after the transaction.

If you have a new offer, product or service, your existing customer base is your best asset and yet many business owners spend untold amounts of money marketing to new customers first.

And worst of all, many of these business owners don't keep a record of their current and past customers so there is no way to market to them.

Major Selling Rule #4

The Offer Is Everything.
What do I mean by everything? Nothing short of being the key to huge immediate profits and ongoing long term success!

In today's world, your offer is the most important part of your advertising. Put another way, the "deal" is everything.

The majority of the success I've had is because of my ability to create an "Irresistible Offer". In the past 9 years, I've taken a very different approach than most experts recommend.

I always perfect my offer before I do anything else with my ads, sales letters, or online marketing.

In today's world, prospects and customers are inundated with advertising. Television, radio, magazines, newspapers, direct mail, the Internet, billboards, movie theaters, grocery stores, and many other sources assault your senses on a daily basis with more advertising than you can possibly absorb.

This means your prospects and customers are numb to advertising. It barely registers anymore.

The way to cut through this saturation and overcome your prospects' disinterest is to make an offer that is so compelling, and so genuine, that it stops them in their tracks and gets the people who have even a mild interest to take notice.

Your offer can't leave anything to the imagination. Every aspect of it should be spelled out in complete detail. It should be impeccably clear and **have an Irresistible Incentive to buy from you right now!**

"The Deal is Everything."

Why Great Copy is Essential

Your website (ALL of your Marketing Materials for that matter) should contain great copy for several reasons. Presenting information the right way is what will get you high search engines rankings.

These high rankings are what will enable people to find you. If you rank near (or at) the top, you will receive more hits than if you rank in the middle or the bottom.

Many web users often don't make it very far down a results page before trying a new search. Most people don't like to search through hundreds of results and simply don't do it.

That is why having a high ranking website is crucial. You want to be seen at the top.

The key is getting several pages to rank high. This allows you to take up several of the spots near the top. This will result in your name and URL being seen multiple times. Users will often click on a name they repeatedly see.

Great website copy presents a call to action. It clearly informs the user of what to do. For example, you might include a page on your website listing the benefits your services provide to your customers.

This should be done in such a way that will prompt them to contact you to learn more. If the benefits are listed very clearly on your page, they should be easy to understand. The same is true for whatever action you want them to take.

Great copy also evokes emotion. You want your visitors to feel something when they go to your site. Many may not be familiar with exactly what services you offer, and upon finding out, may feel a particular emotion.

Perhaps it's hope or maybe even excitement because they finally found the information they need. No matter what it is, you have made a difference for them. While it is about what you say, it's also about how you say it.

Your web copy should also tell compelling stories. These can come in the form of testimonials. People often respond well upon hearing about the experiences of others. You might even explain why you decided to open your business and tell readers about your expertise in the field.

When writing your copy, tell your stories in a way that will speak directly to your visitors. This is one of the easiest ways to turn a prospect into a customer.

This is also a great way to gain trust. Prospects will want to come to you if they feel you know what you are doing and will take good care of them.

Your website copy is what will help establish your online credibility. You must write content that will inform, convince, identify with your visitor, and inspire a particular action to be taken. This often leads to the sharing of such information.

A visitor who has become a customer may then recommend others to visit your website and, ultimately, your business.

Your online presence should expand your business. It can help you reach people who aren't in close proximity to you, but who might greatly benefit from the services you have to offer.

7 Internet Marketing Strategies To Drive Traffic To Your Business

There are 7 major strategies for creating a dominating local online presence. We will discuss each in great detail in the following chapters. When properly executed each of the strategies can bring new customers to your Local Business. When you combine these strategies you create a formidable presence for your business.

Strategy 1: Search Engine Optimization

Search Engine Optimization (SEO) makes a website more desirable to the search engines and optimized websites are seen at the top.

The main ways to optimize a website are through creating great content, specific keywords that are searched for on a regular basis, interaction on your website from people visiting and you also want to have other sites pointing to your website (which is called back linking).

When Google or one of the other search engine crawls (looks at) a website and it sees that there are other reputable websites (referred to as authority sites) that have links pointing to your website, they go, "Hey, other sites think this is important, so this site must be important," and it moves the site up the search rankings.

The other important key is to have links out to other high-ranking authority sites like CNN, YouTube, etc. When the search engines see that your site is pointing to some of these other high ranking sites that have great information it helps to move your site up in the rankings.

The other part about SEO is using keywords. What are the words that you want to show up for when people are searching? When it comes to Local Marketing, it's not as hard as you may think. You can ask the first 10 people you run into, "if you were looking for a dentist in Denver, what would you type in to the search engine?" More than likely if you ask 10 people, those are the top 10 things that people would probably search for.

With Local Marketing that's about as complicated as you need to get with keyword research. Now, there are a lot of tools out there that can go very in-depth but I would say you could very easily use the keyword tool that's available in any search engine to look at how many searches people are actually doing and how strong the competition is.

Previously the majority of website rankings were based on technical attributes. Things like On-page SEO, overuse of keywords (keyword stuffing), backlinks etc. previously helped your websites ranking. Now Content Creation is King.

Google is now friendlier to original content than purchased traffic. The search engines use an ever-changing algorithm to determine what shows up on the first page. Today they reward originality of quality content and visitor interaction (time on site) more so than the number or backlinks.

Keyword Research – What Are Your Prospects Looking For?

Keywords are the foundation of SEO. Keywords are the exact terms consumers are using to find what they are searching for. Single keywords are too broad of a search term for local searches. Three to Five words together are known as "long tail keyword phrases" are more powerful for local searches since they usually include a geographic identifier. These are usually used for very specific searches and have higher conversions.

Optimizing your website with long tail keywords is very important. By placing 4 to 6 long tail keywords in your website's code and in the page titles can help your website ranking. An example of a single keyword would be the term "Acupuncture". An example of a long tail keyword would be "Pain Management Acupuncture Clinic Casper, WY". As you can tell someone using the single keyword is looking for general information on Acupuncture. The person using the long tail keyword phrase is going to find specific results for a Pain Management Acupuncture clinic in Casper, WY.

When creating content for Facebook, Twitter, blogs, YouTube, etc. always use your keywords in the title first. Content Creation with relevant keywords will help your website's organic ranking, and remember to avoid overstuffing. Overstuffing is excessive use of keywords and is frowned upon by search engines.

A great way to find out the best keywords to use for your website or content is by using Google's free keyword tool. You can research your specific keywords and it will make suggestions of keyword terms that are closely related to your search terms. The keyword planner will show you how many searches each term gets per month. This can help you identify the best terms to use so that the most people will see your information. It will also show you which keywords are rated low, medium and highly competitive. This is important because it will be easier to rank for the low to medium competition keywords.

Strategy 2 - Incoming Links

Quality incoming links are still **one of the single biggest ranking factors** that Google looks at when deciding just how high your pages, websites, videos, blogs and any other online content should rank in their search results. An incoming link is when another website "links" to yours. The higher the quality of the site linking to you, the more "Link Juice" you will get. i.e. if you are a Doctor and you get WebMd to link to an article you wrote! Bam! Massive Link Juice

Strategy 3: Pay Per Click Advertising

Advertising on Google with Google Adwords is done by placing your ads in front of people who are actively searching for a term or "keyword" related to your product of service.

You are charged each time someone clicks on your ad. When they click on your ad it takes them to the web page you want them to see that will lead them to an Involvement and making a purchase from you.

Let's look at an example of a company that sells Pool Supplies. They want their ads to show up in front of people who are actively searching for information about "pool supplies". We don't know exactly what type of information they are looking for, we just know they are they are searching the term "Austin Pool Supplies".

The ads show up at the Top of the Results page and along the right hand side of the page similar to Facebook ads. The results in the middle of the page are organic search results. These are important but we will save that for a different time.

When someone gets the result for searching "Austin Pool Supplies" they have the option of clicking on the links that most appeal to them. There is no guarantee that your ad will get clicked, you have to have a great headline, and body content that intrigues the prospect.

The 7 Steps to Set Up a Winning Adwords Campaign

1 - Set Your Goals

You will want to determine exactly what you're looking to achieve with your campaign. Do you want a specific number of leads per month? Are you looking to increase inbound phone calls, newsletter signups, or make sales on your web site?

2 - Do Your Research

Research the Keywords – Use keyword tools like Market Samurai or Google's Keyword Planner to find the most relevant keywords people are typing into the search engines to find your product/service/company.

Research Your Competition – You will want to spend some time looking at the competition to see who consistently is ranking at or near the top of the rankings (you can use a spy tool like Keyword Spy Tool to help). Pay attention to their ad copy and offers. Visit their websites. Sign up for their mailing lists. Purchase their products.

Research Your Audience – Where are customers buying and reviewing products/services/businesses like yours online? Take a look at the reviews they are posting. What do they love/hate about your competition? What are the needs or desires they are looking to fulfill? While doing this part of the research you should be on the look out for great quotes you can use for ad copy.

3 The Landing Page/Offer

An irresistible offer on your landing page is the absolute keystone to your AdWords campaign. While you were doing your research you saw what all your top competitors are offering. Now all you have to do is make your offer just a little bit unique, different or better? It is amazing what just a small improvement over the competition can make! (This is also usually the beginning of an Automated Sales Funnel!)

4 Use Exact Match Keywords

When first starting out with AdWords, you will want your keyword list very small (5 – 10 keywords) and very focused (the ones that people who are ready to buy are most likely to be typing into Google). Add all these keywords to your campaign as Exact Match keywords (this means that your ads will only be shown when someone types that exact term into Google).

This way your ads will only show up for the most relevant searches and not for variations that Google may think are relevant, but aren't.

Over time, you can eliminate the keywords that aren't getting clicks or conversions and expand on the ones that are.

For example, if "Denver Dentist" is working for you, add more Exact Match variations of it to the list. Do this by combining the word "Dentist" with zip codes, nearby cities, and by using variations like "Dentists near Denver, CO", "best Dentist in Denver", etc.

5 Use Unique and Proven Ads

The ad copy should be highly relevant to the keywords they show up for (including the exact terms when possible). Make sure you stand out from the competition by using different offers, benefits, etc. Your landing page/offer should also reflect the same messaging as your ads to help people feel they are in the right place. (If you landing page is not consistent with your ad copy it will hurt your conversions.

Test your ads. To do this you will place at least 2 ads in each ad group and then split test them. As a general rule of thumb, after each ad has at least 30 clicks, delete the lower performing ad and replace it with a new one.

6 Track Your Results

Whatever the goals for your campaign, track your results.

Track downloads, newsletter signups, sales, etc. with AdWords conversion tracking. If phone calls are what you're after, use a Call Tracking service.

7 Mine the Data

You get data from AdWords you can't get anywhere else. Take advantage of it.

You can use the keyword data to find keywords that are good candidates for Search Engine Optimization (SEO) for your website.

As mentioned above, test different messages, headlines and offers in your ads. When you find ones that people really respond to, test them on your landing pages and in other marketing media.

Used this way the information you get from AdWords and Facebook Ads can be the fuel that runs your entire marketing engine.

Adwords Campaign Basics

Adwords Takes Time

1 Week to Research and Build a Solid Account
1 Month to Establish a Solid Baseline
3+ Months to Optimize

Adwords Cost Money

A budget appropriate for your industry to obtain a minimum of 100 clicks a month. This can range from $300 to $30,000 depending on your industry. A lesser budget will result in too little data that is not statistically significant.

Lack of data will delay your ability to make timely optimizations and prove profitability.

Adwords Policies Change

Policy changes can affect your camper resulting in at this approvals or site suspensions.

Policy updates can occur at any time without notice.

All advertisers are not created equal when it comes to policies and websites are subject to random annual review.

Objectives and Measurement of Adwords Campaigns

Lead Generation
Ecommerce
Branding
Event Tracking
Incoming Call Tracking

Types of Call Tracking

Static Number Placed on a webpage
Dynamic Number Insertion
Keyword Level Tracking
Call Recording

How Dynamic Number Insertion works

Requires a small snippet of JavaScript to be added to the head of your website.

When someone clicks on a paid search ad, the code replaces your business phone number with the specific tracking number.

The calls made to the tracking number can be recorded.

Keyword level data can be tracked if you append your AdWords URL with the keyword tracking parameter.

Implementing the Code

Should be implemented by your webmaster.

Code is pasted in the top of your website, after the <head> tag of each page.

Call Extensions

Call extensions allow your phone number to be displayed with your ad.

Call extensions are required to enable the click to "call ad" option on mobile devices.

These calls are defined as pre-click phone calls.

Call Extension Tracking

Calls can be tracked by using Google forwarding but Google cannot record calls.

Google has recently changed their policy which requires the phone number in the call extension to be verified on your website.

This made it impossible to use your dynamically insert a tracking number in your extension and impossible to record these calls.

We created a workaround! We have developed a small snippet of code that allows us to hide the tracking number on the site around Google to verify it to see it only if they arrive from an AdWords ad.

Lead Generation Goal

KPI – CPA (Cost Per Acquisition)

Based on the amount of leads it takes the business to close a sale and the average value of each sale and lifetime value.

Ecommerce Goal

KPI – ROAS (return on ad spend).

Based on average profit margin of goods sold, type of products (consumable or non) and lifetime value.

Calculating Realistic Goals

A roofer with a CPA goal of $20

> Your keyword research predicts average CPC will be $7.50.

> Average conversion rate for a well-built landing page is 10%

1 Lead = 10 clicks x $7.50
1 Lead = $75

Initial Campaign Default Goals

Lead Generation - 10% Conversion Rate
Ecommerce - 2:1 ROAS
CTR - should be 2.5 which is slightly above average

Determine Your True Competitors

There is likely a difference between who you think your competitors are and who your competitors actually are.

Perform a Google search for keywords you would use to find your business.

Research the competitors that appear in the ads, organic listings, map and other Google results.

Adwords Ad Competition

Does the competition appear to be high?

Is the SERP filled with ads?

Do the competitors ads have a unique value proposition?

How does this compare to your business?

What is the size of the competition?

Will you be competing against Walmart, Amazon or other national retail service franchises?

Website Experience

Does their website have a unique value proposition?

Is the contact information easy to find?

Do they have a clear call to action?

How does this compare to your business?

It All comes Down To You

Compare your competitors Value Proposition and website to yours.

Who would you most likely want to do business with?

If the answer is your competition, you will need to improve yours to improve your chance of having a profitable PPC campaign.

Strategy 4: Put Your Business In Your Prospects Pocket

Local Online directories are web properties that allow businesses to list the details of their business at no cost. These directories can be vitally important for any Local Businesses. These listings can show up in the online search results and on apps on mobile phones like CitySearch, Google Maps, Yelp, and many more.

The reason this is critical for any Local Business is that according to a comScore-Localeze survey, 50% of Local Searches on mobile devices are done using these Directory Apps.

It's like every person with a smart phone is walking around with access to 15 different phone books at their disposal at any second, right in the palm of their hand!

So which one is it most important to be listed in?...
The simple answer is all of them!

Google+ Local is the largest local directory on the Internet. It actually gives information for Local Business as a listing in Google.

This allows clients a way to actually show up on the first page of Google whenever someone searches for their industry and city.

If you put in "Denver Dentist," as I mentioned earlier, it will show up with Dentists in Denver that are on a map shown on Google.

Google+ Local is the way for any Local Business to put information online and have it show up on the first page.

Many business owners are not as familiar with Google+ as they are with other social media websites. However, with approximately 343 million active users, the site is gaining in popularity and should be considered as part of your marketing plan.

One of the most popular aspects of Google+ is that it allows users to create circles. These circles can include friends, businesses, work colleagues, and customers. By creating different circles for each of these groups, you can then share specific information with a specific circle.

This technique allows you to create customer and business related content that you can then share in the respective circle. This is a great way for businesses to tailor their marketing plan to reach their target market using Google+.

Another benefit that Google+ offers is that it allows you to share coupons, announce new products, host contests, share blog posts, and publicize current promotions.

This is a great way for businesses to share information that is relevant to their existing clients and helpful in attracting new ones.

Businesses also have the opportunity to use their Google+ page as a way to humanize their business. This can be done by sharing videos or stories about your employees and what they do each day.

In addition to the benefits we have already mentioned, another important benefit to using Google+ is that it can have a positive effect on your online visibility.

When people interact with your Google+ page or +1 your content, it is demonstrating to Google that people are interested in your business.

When Google notices this, they will begin to reward your activity on Google+ with a higher search engine ranking.

This means that when people search for a product or service that you offer, you will become easier to find and be placed closer to the top of the search results provided.

Another way that being an active member on Google+ can help your business is that when your posts are properly optimized, Google will take notice.

To ensure that your posts are properly optimized, you should include keywords and topics that relate to your specific business niche.

When optimizing your content, it is important that you include these terms in your content naturally.

If you include too many keywords, or they do not flow organically they may have the opposite effect. Keep your content natural and organic and you will get the attention of Google.

Google+ is a valuable marketing tool for any business. If you are already using social media as part of your marketing plan you should consider what Google+ has to offer. It is a great way to increase awareness about your business and attract new clients.

How To Get Google+ Reviews For Your Business

A Google+ listing for your business is an integral part of your internet reputation. It will be an invaluable tool for your online marketing plan. One essential factor is reviews.

Customer reviews can make or break you; they are what often provide others with the information to make a decision. You want plenty of positive reviews in order to make the most out of your Google+ listing.

The reviews you receive should be relevant, high quality customer accounts. So how do you handle this aspect of your Google+ listing? Below are some tips that will get you started; these tips will show you how to get reviews as well as respond to them.

Ask for positive reviews. This is simple. If you have satisfied customers, encourage them to visit your Google+ listing and write a review. Explain how easy it is to do and won't take very long. They will only need to click on the "write a review" button located at the top left corner of your listing and begin typing.

Google+ provides you with a link that is personalized just for your business. You can send it to your email and/or regular postal mail lists for the purpose of directing people to your listing. When doing this, be sure to ask for reviews.

You should also include this link on all business correspondence as well as ads and marketing materials. This is another great way to promote your link and request reviews.

List your business in directories such as: Bing, Yelp, and Yahoo. Business listings, Foursquare, and all other reviews that are submitted to those sites will be automatically linked to and will show up on your Google+ listing.

Responding to reviews is just as important as receiving them. Feedback is very important and can go both ways. Below are more useful tips. Unfortunately, there will always be people who are unhappy with your business no matter what you do. Sometimes these people will be unhappy with any business. Still, you will want to respond in a way that will preserve your reputation. Responding is the way to do this.

Respond promptly. This will show the negative reviewers you are paying attention to what they had to say. Make an attempt through your response to resolve any existing issues. Express your perspective in a way that isn't insulting or self-justifying.

You will, of course, get plenty of positive reviews. Always be sure to thank your satisfied customers for their support. In the case of your business, tell your customers how much you appreciate their great reviews.

You might also offer public referral rewards and coupons to customers through the Google Plus listing forum.

This will encourage potential customers to pay you a visit.

There are dozens of local directories available to any Local Business and in order for a listing to show up in the search results it must be consistently optimized similar to Google+ above. Each directory listing needs to have pictures and videos. The description of the business needs to be written exactly the right way. The features of the business and the categories all need to be listed in such a way that it gets the attention of local searchers. This allows you to show your hours of operation and directions to your location. People can push one button to call the store or get turn-by-turn directions from where they are straight to you front door.

Another powerful part of Local Directories are citations created by people leaving reviews of their experience with your business. Obviously, the higher the ratings and reviews, the more people like it, right?

Think about the last thing you bought on Amazon, I'll bet you looked at the ratings other people had given the book or product. The same thing goes for your Local Business!

Strategy 5: Social Media

Facebook, Twitter, YouTube and More

The next traffic path is social media. There are a ton of these sites on the Internet and everyone looks at Facebook and Twitter as the two biggest players online. And for good reason, **Facebook has over 1.4 Billion users and Twitter has over 300 Million active tweeters.**

These platforms provide channels for getting information in front of huge amounts of people. You can identify them and target them locally based on the geographic information; on both of those systems, people tell you what they do, what they like and where they live (most of the time).

Facebook is more social. You can advertise and put a wider variety of information there. Twitter is about marketing to the masses and small little bursts called tweets.

With Twitter, you can only post a message that's 140 characters in length. With 140 characters, you don't have a lot of room to go into a detailed description. You can target your audience with tools like twellow.com to identify people who are in the city that you're dealing with.

Facebook provides a lot more demographic information on its users, which allows you to target your audience based on location, age, gender, relationship status, education, profession, and interests. Armed with this information you can develop ad campaigns and have them presented only to your ideal client.

Retargeting or Re-Marketing Tracking Pixels

Retargeting is a cookie-based technology that simply uses a Javascript code to anonymously 'follow' your audience all over the internet.

Here's how it works: you place a small, unobtrusive piece of code on your website (this code is sometimes referred to as a pixel).

The code, or pixel, is unnoticeable to your site visitors and won't affect your site's performance. Every time a new visitor comes to your site, the code drops an anonymous browser cookie.

Later, when your cookied visitors browses the Web, the cookie will let your retargeting provider know when to serve ads, ensuring that your ads are served only to people who have previously visited your site.

It helps you:

- Bring back website visitors to complete a purchase.

- Find new people who are similar to your website visitors.

- Get more value from your new customer acquisition campaigns by excluding existing customers.

For instance, if you were doing a golf ad, you would definitely want to cut the demographics down to your Target Market. Let's say, you wanted to target female golfers in Denver, Colorado. You would probably select, obviously, females. You would select a range of probably 25 to 55. You might select college educated. And you would probably select married. This should all be based on solid research on your market demographics.

Another aspect of social media is YouTube, and I'll talk about that a little bit more when I get into the video section, but YouTube is actually a social media platform because you can have subscribers, send messages, and leave comments. YouTube is the second largest search engine in the world behind Google. Google owns Youtube.

LinkedIn is a social networking site designed specifically for the business community. The goal of the site is to allow registered members to establish networks of people they know and trust professionally. The owner of the business must have a LinkedIn profile, and the business must have a company profile. There are some social aspects to LinkedIn, but it's really about business. Business owners, salespeople, and business professionals.

The main goal of all these sites is to direct people to your website, so make sure you are always leading them there.

On most social sites you can optimize profiles for Local Business. With Facebook you can set up a Facebook fan page, create a customized time line and create content for people to interact with. For a restaurant you could post pictures of the menu items; if it's a Doctor's office, you might display before and after pictures of services. You want them to be a fan of the page and ultimately become a customer of the business, product or service.

You can customize the background on Twitter, customize the feed, and customize the information you provide to your followers. The information that the business owner provides should be useful to the person who's viewing it whether they choose to do business with them or not. I'll reiterate this point a few times because it really is the key factor when it comes to creating a credible presence online.

The Power of Video

Video is one of the most powerful means of putting information online. Why? Well, ask yourself this. What do people do more often, read books or watch television? Obviously, it's watch television because most people don't want to read. They're lazy and they like to be entertained.

If you look at YouTube, what are the videos that have the most views? They are entertaining, or they are providing information. They entertain; they're funny or controversial.

Now, the other videos that get a lot of views are videos that provide great information in a way that gets people's attention.

For instance, if you do a search on Google or YouTube to figure out what causes the popping sound when you crack your neck, back or knuckles, you will find a Chiropractor answering the question, "What's that popping sound?" It has over 257,444 views. That's because people want to know what that popping sound is when the Chiropractor adjusts them.

Whenever you answer questions that people want know, it increases the video ranking. When you post a video you want to be sure to title it with the information of how people will search for it.

For instance, going back to our "Dentist in Denver" example, you would want to put "Denver Dentist Explains Why Root Canals Hurt." That way you have the geographic identifier, you have the Dentist part, and then you have what the description of the content. You also want to put in keywords and tags so that it gets people's attention and can possibly show up in the search engines.

The real value of video is having people find it in local searches, and it also provides you with tons of content that you can use to post on social media platforms.

What we've discovered is there are a lot of different ways to make videos. You can use animoto.com where you simply put pictures in, and it will actually add music and create a video for you. You can make videos using PowerPoint or Keynote, which is like PowerPoint for Mac.

The simplest and easiest way to make a video is to use the camera on your phone and record yourself answering questions that you get asked all time. These are called frequently asked questions. When you post these FAQ videos you will see favorable results, because people are usually looking for answers to these questions online.

Videos are very search engine friendly and can rank on the first page rather quickly with the right title and tags. Of course YouTube is the biggest video sharing site and the second largest search engine on the planet so it is very important to have your videos uploaded there, but YouTube is not the only player in town.

It is also very beneficial to put videos on other video sharing sites like Vimeo, Viddler, Kewego, and more. There's a ton of them out there. You can simply do a Google search for video sharing sites, and you'll get an entire list of all the places that you can post videos.

Using YouTube to Market Your Business

Getting Started – To get started using YouTube, you will first need to create your channel. This step may require a little time, but the effort you put into creating and customizing the channel to suit your business will be well worth it.

When you customize your channel, you should include your logo and customize the colors to those related to your logo and business. This will give your channel a customized look and help it be recognized by those familiar with your brand.

During the initial setup phase, you should include the option of allowing users to subscribe to your channel. This will ensure that your target market is receiving your latest videos.

Types of Videos – Now that you've created your channel, you're probably wondering what types of videos to begin posting. The best types of videos for businesses tend to be how-to videos and FAQ videos. These types of videos will allow you to show your subscribers how to use your products in the most effective manner.

You can also show uses for your products that your customers may not be aware of. How-to and FAQ videos are also a great way to drive traffic to your website.

Sharing – When you create your YouTube channel, you will then be able to share your videos across your other social media pages. Posting your videos on your Facebook page is a great way to show your customers that you are on YouTube and that your videos have something to offer. You can also share links to your videos in your tweets and email, which will help expand your subscribers to your YouTube channel.

Feedback – Each time that you post a new video, you can gain valuable feedback. Your customers will be able to leave comments about your video, products, or tips that you included in your video. This is a great way for you to see what is working and what you may need to change.

Online Visibility – YouTube is also a great way for businesses to increase their online visibility. When someone searches for a product or service that you offer or have mentioned in a video, your link will be presented in those search results.

To truly benefit from this, you should be sure to include relevant keywords in your video titles. This will help increase the visibility of your videos and gain valuable exposure for your business.

Increasing Involvement of Your Videos!

What is Involvement?

Involvement is the interaction between the viewer and the video creator or between the viewer and the video itself.

Involvement is measured by the number and type of actions taken by viewers.

– Comments

- Likes

– Subscribes

– Shares

– Adding your videos to their Playlists – Favorites

Why Is Involvement Important!

• YouTube's rewards video creators who's content attracts "engaged" viewers (reward, as in get more free traffic).

• Involvement actions are viral by nature and help attract even more free traffic.

The Number One Rule Of Involvement...

If you want a viewer to do something, ask them to do it and then tell them HOW to do it using these 6 Tips.

Involvement Tip 1

- Write your video scripts so they encourage viewer Involvement. – "Speak to the viewer" in a conversational way

- Feature viewer comments and video responses in your own video

- Ask their opinion

- Ask specific questions that require more than a simple "yes or no" from them to answer

- Ask them to share your videos with their friends

- Ask them to leave comments,subscribe,favorite and leave comments – Ask them to watch more of your content and tell them how to do it.

Involvement Tip 2

Add Call to Action annotations to your videos encouraging them to engage with your content.

- Leave comments and feedback
- Subscribe to your channel
- Add your video to their Playlists
- Like and Favorite your video
- Share your video on social networks or with their email lists

Involvement Tip 3

Add Call to Action links that make it easier for them to watch more of your content.

- Link to your Playlists
- Link to your other Videos
- Link to Your Subscribe Button
- Link to Your Channel
- Include Links In Your Annotations

Involvement Tip 4

Insert an annotation just before the point where the average viewer stops watching that encourages them to engage with the video and/or to continue watching.

"Average view duration" inside YouTube Analytics

Involvement Tip 5

Design Your Annotations So They Stand Out From The Page So Viewers Can Easily Spot Them. Design y

Involvement Tip 6

Insert Involvement Calls To Actions And Involvement Links In Your Video Descriptions.

YouTube Stats

- 4 Billion Views a Day
- Each Second 1 Hour of Video is Uploaded
- Each Month there are 800 Million Users
- YouTube has had over 1 Trillion Views
- YouTube Mobile has 600 Million Views Each Day
- Google bought YouTube in 2006 for $1.65 Billion

Strategy 6: Mobile Mass Marketing

Why is mobile marketing becoming so important? Well, let me ask you a question. Do you have a mobile device within arm's reach that you can access the Internet with? Go ahead. Think about it. I'll wait... Of course you do. Right now, within three feet of you, you probably have your cell phone. And that cell phone probably is a Smartphone... And that Smartphone has the ability to get online. You have a way of searching the web from nearly any mobile device.

When someone does a local search on a mobile device they usually make a purchase based on the information they find within 24 hours vs. a week or longer from a search on a computer. For restaurants it is usually within 60 minutes...

That is what we call a purchase driven consumer!

With mobile marketing there are a couple of ways to market information. The first is by creating a mobile website. If you look at a regular website on your iPhone or Android, a lot of times they're jumbled up. They may look like it does online, but the screen is really small and you have to pinch and squeeze and move stuff around. And it's hard to navigate.

A mobile site really takes your website, cuts it down to about four or five pages of the most relevant information. That way, when someone goes to that website, they are able to navigate it very quickly. For instance, if it's a restaurant, it would have a contact us button, a menu button, a directions button, and maybe a "specials" button so that they can get to just the information that they're looking for.

For example, for a restaurant website should have a takeout menu, because most people, when they go on their phone looking for food, it's takeout.

Another way to utilize mobile marketing is with SMS or text messages. With text marketing, you have to first capture the subscriber's phone number, and then you can then market to them over time using text messages.

Why is mobile advertising so important? Well here's the thing: only about 36% of emails get opened compared to over 92% of text messages or mobile messages get looked at within the first minutes of being received.

As a matter of fact, you've probably looked at your phone while you've been reading this report. That's the power of mobile marketing.

Using a Mobile App to Showcase Your Business

Yep... There's an app for that...

And today many Local Businesses are taking advantage of having an app made just for their business. A mobile app is a software application developed specifically for use on a wireless device like a smartphone or tablet rather than a desktop or laptop computer. The applications are housed on and made available on Apple and Google Play.

A mobile app for your business gives your customers the opportunity to have your business information loaded directly on their smartphones so they can interact with your business and receive specific communications.

Having a Customized App Allows Businesses To:

Build Customer Loyalty

Make your customers feel special by offering discounts, coupons, and promotions just for using your app.

Send Push Notifications

Deliver instant messages to your customers' mobile phones whenever you wish. While only 4% to 10% of emails get opened, push notifications get read 97% of the time.

Create Viral Buzz

Let customers quickly tell all of their friends about you using the built-in sharing capabilities of Facebook, Twitter, LinkedIn, your blog, SMS, and Email.

Grow Your List

Gather names and email addresses directly inside your app and easily export them into your favorite email marketing campaign service.

Promote Special Events

Provide up-to-date information about all of your business events, sales, and promotions with an in-app events calendar that anyone can access.

Gain More Credibility

These are still the early years of the mobile app. Having one adds serious credibility to your business—especially among those who don't know how easy we make it.

Keep Customers Informed

Fill your app with information about your business, service offerings, product samples, menus, and more. There's a tab for just about everything you want them to know.

Connect With Ease

Make it simple for customers to reach you using one touch calling, email, a website link, and GPS directions to to your business—all from inside your app

Get Instant Feedback

Allow customers to leave feedback on your fan wall, share photos, make restaurant reservations, and send comments in a variety of ways.

Track Your Success

Use robust analytics to track daily, weekly, and monthly downloads of your app.

MOBILE STATS

- 50% of Consumers use their smart phones to find Local Businesses.

- Mobile Phones will be used more then PC's

- Over half of consumers use their phones in stores for buying decisions.

- In 1-year smartphones users will be over 1 billion worldwide.

- Mobile is predicted to be bigger then the Internet in 2 years.

- Over 70%+ of online retailers are developing a mobile strategy.

- Smart phone market is now bigger than the PC market.

Strategy 7: Blogging

When most people think about blogging they think of a site focused on topics with a national scope. Locally focused blogs are powerful marketing tools for smart business owners. The power of the blog comes from the focus on the local community, which provides ample opportunities to use the city or town in the blog post headlines.

Blogs are very easy to create using one of the popular sites like Word Press or Blogger and with proper keyword placement the blog posts can easily rank on the first page of the search engines. Make sure your content has value to the audience you are trying to attract and be careful not to overload the posts with too many keywords.

Always post a variety of content that your audience will find interesting. If you only post information about your business and products & services you will lose the interest of most readers. Look for other local bloggers and offer them guest-posting opportunities on your blog.

If Jay Leno were the only person on the Tonight Show it would eventually get boring... Jay is an entertaining guy but the guests on his show are what add the variety that keeps it interesting.

Use pictures on your blog. People are very visual in nature and a blog post with pictures get more interaction and than text only posts. You can also name the picture files with the keyword to increase optimization for the post.

Always ask for feedback. Involvement is very important with local audiences. Challenge your audience with questions and ask them to leave their answers and comments.

This Involvement will not only make things more interesting for the readers, it will also make the post more relevant to the search engines and you will be rewarded with better search rankings.

Direct Response Marketing

How to Get More Business Without Having to Get More Customers...

The fortune is in... The Fish bowl?
Not the thing you were expecting right? Think about it... you go into a restaurant and they have a fish bowl on the counter at the register for you to drop in a business card to enter to win a free appetizer, lunch, dessert, or maybe even free drinks.

What do you think happens to those cards after the remove them from the fish bowl?

NOTHING!
I can tell you from experience.

At this point you may be thinking that's great but we don't have a fish bowl on our front counter. And you are right... But... EVERY business has a fish bowl, they just don't sit at the register and they don't look like fish bowls.

Remember the last time you went to the Dentist or Doctor and saw those patient folders along the wall behind the receptionist with the colored tabs on them? **Fish Bowl!**

Ever go into a business that had rows of customer files in file cabinets along a wall?   **Fish Bowl!**

Oil Change companies put that little sticker on your windshield...
Fish Bowl!

Excel spreadsheets with customer invoices and contact info...
Fish Bowl!

EVERY business that collects contact information from their customers has a Fish bowl! Those customers willingly gave you their information and it is your job... your responsibility to tell them when you have an offer that they might find interesting.

Staying in touch with your customers is easier than you think!

There are very simple and inexpensive services called auto-responders that you can use to set up your client lists and send out communications to your customer base with the touch of a button.

These systems can send email, text messages and some can even send recorded phone messages.

Email Marketing - Why an Automated Email Engine is Essential

These days, there are greater time constrictions on businesses which act to limit consistent marketing. Many of the limitations are due, in part, to fewer staff and tighter budgets. One of the greatest strategies to oppose this challenge is with the use of automated email systems for your business or clinic. These routine reminders are great for increasing website traffic and general sales.

Local Businesses have seen tremendous results from this line of promotion and have abandoned antiquated and far more time consumptive methods of keeping in touch with clients. Understanding that workforce cutbacks and reduced line item funds for constant contacts are far more the norm than the exception, many companies have even eliminated them altogether. If you find your company with staff that plays dual roles, you understand the importance of managing time and labor.

The controlled management of your sales process is crucial. An effective way of administrating this process is through maintenance with preset systems that contact your entire population. Many of these systems have tracking and progress reporting as a regular function.

You can either go with an experienced company, or hire an IT professional to build an individualized program that best meets your center's needs.

There is a popular saying that declares, "...if you build it-they will come." It might be wise to add that if it is built and never used or disseminated, they will turn and go in another direction. Do not shoot your business success in the foot by making the mistake of inadequately using the system in which you invested.

Make certain that the email addresses of all your clients are current. Have it be part of the process when they enter your business for scheduled visits. Check regularly to see which messages are returned and eliminate those addresses.

It is encouraged to send out several reminders or informative messages. Your clients may not participate or purchase from the first contact, but they may just be ready when the next one arrives.

Build the opportunity for client suggestions and feedback into the message. Tag a staff member to be responsible for responding to the comments.

These responses should be done in a timely manner. It could mean the difference between a happy customer and a lost one.

After you have had some time to track and monitor the impact of your businesses automated promotions system, don't just sit on the information.

Take the time to let it guide and instruct your marketing future. Did it meet your contact needs?

Did you see an increase to your website visits? Did you see an increase in visits to your physical location or the sale of a particular product?

These strategies are not only save time and cost; they work to inform your marketing practices and processes.

You will only enhance the good work and for which your center is known. You will also give your clients the consistent and careful service and information they deserve.

Behavioral Dynamic Response Marketing
by Frank Kern

(One of my mentors, Frank Kern, taught me about Behavioral Dynamic Response Marketing and it is what we use for all of my businesses and what I build for my consulting clients. Below is how he describes it.)

Behavioral Dynamic Response Marketing is the automated process of giving unique and specific content to prospects and customers based on their actions.

It's giving your audience a personalized experience based on what they do and don't do and when they do or don't do it.

In a world where most prospects and customers see the same marketing and sales messages over and over and over, it makes more sense to give each person uniquely tailored messages that apply to them based on their previous actions.

We use in my businesses and build for our consulting clients, multi-phased <u>campaigns</u>, that are all centered around and consider **"Behavioral Response Indicators."**

In every sales situation, there is always an action or series of actions a prospect usually takes before they buy. We call these Behavioral Response Indicators.

Here's how this applies to you...

Let's say you're advertising a free report in exchange for the prospect's email.

And let's assume that in order for the prospect to trust you enough to buy, they need to read the very report they've opted in for.

The act of reading your report is a Behavioral Response Indicator.

Research shows that over 50% of prospects never consume the information they opt in for.

They're basically saying "no" to the thing they just requested.

This means your chances of getting the sale immediately are cut in half because half of your prospects never made it through the first Behavioral Response Indicator.

The way you fix this is by creating sequences in your campaigns who's sole purpose is to move your prospect from one response indicator to the next ...until they buy.

And the way you do that is to incorporate Behavioral Dynamic Response systems into everything you do.

It works by tracking what your prospects are doing in your campaign, and then dynamically sending them customized marketing messages based on their behavior.

I recently created a video designed to attract clients who were interested in having my company create and deploy their marketing campaigns for them.

The video walked people through exactly how to create a winning campaign, and offered them the ability to apply to talk with my office at the end.

These are the initial Behavioral Response Indicators for that campaign:

1. Begin the video.

2. Finish the video. (So they would then see my offer).

3. Apply to speak with us about becoming a client.

The campaign had to be designed to get as many people through those Behavioral Response Indicators as possible.

The first thing I did was to track how many people were beginning the video.

If they didn't start the video, I send them email reminders to go and watch it.

Their access to the video is only available for three days.

If they didn't start the video they opted in for, they would get email reminders telling them their access was about to expire.

Our software also dynamically calculated the date their access would expire, and merged that date into the reminder emails for added incentive.

Instead of saying, "your access expires in three days", the email would say, "your access expires on Friday the 30th."

This one little mechanism is a huge deal.

All because we identified the first Behavioral Response Indicator and created a specialized sequence that tracked their behavior and responded accordingly.

If all other factors in the campaign remained constant, we just achieved a 50% increase in sales from this one small tweak.

But this was just the start.

The next Behavioral Response Indicator was to get them to finish the entire video and see my offer.

As you know, video is quickly becoming the primary way people consume content online.

And if you're using it to sell your services or products, your viewers need to watch the whole video so you can make your entire case.

According to Wistia, less than half of video viewers make it through videos that are only two minutes long.

Go longer than two minutes and it gets even worse.

Here's how I accomplished the impossible, and how you can model my system.

Always track what your prospects are doing and respond accordingly.

In this campaign, I kept track of how much of the video they actually watched.

If they leave before finishing, my email engine sends them emails telling them what they were missing ...and sending them back to go watch the rest.

In other words, my system automatically tracks their behavior ...and then dynamically responds by sending them customized messages to get them through to the next step in the campaign.

I built special follow-up sequences to go out if they leave before the 10 minute mark, the 20 minute, and the end.

Each sequence was a little different ...referencing what'd they'd seen and telling them what they'd missed ...based on how far along they'd gotten in the video ...and telling them to go finish it.

By doing this, I was able to get most people to finish the video.

Again, the three Behavioral Response Indicators were to get them to:

A: Start the video.

B: Watch the whole video.

C: Apply to speak with my office about building their campaigns for them.

We did a great job of getting through the first two steps.

They were starting the video, watching the whole thing.

But there was a problem.

Even though they loved the video, only 2% of them who finished it were applying to talk to us about becoming clients.
At first glance, this is ok because our services aren't cheap and they're certainly not for everyone.

And I was very up front about price in the video.

Most people would be very happy with a 2% "conversion rate" at our price point.

But that wasn't enough.

I don't settle for "acceptable" or even "good". I insist on exceptional.

If the video got a 2% conversion, that means 98% of the people who saw it said "NO" to my offer at the end.

But they didn't say "no" because they weren't interested, and they didn't say "no" because they didn't want the outcome I could help them achieve.

If that were the case, they wouldn't have stayed for the entire video.

In a situation where prospects go through your campaign, read your messages, watch your videos, and still say "no" it's almost always for one of these reasons:

1. Plain old fashioned laziness.

Many of your prospects won't buy because they didn't feel like getting up, finding their wallet, digging out their credit card, and then typing in all that information.

2. Procrastination.

They are interested and they want the outcome, but they're distracted by something and tell themselves they'll get to it later.

3. And finally, they need for more information.

They're almost ready to buy but they just need some extra push. They've got a question, or a concern, or might just need a little more time to make a decision.

These Are The People Who Will Make You The Most Money.

You know they're interested because they have behaviorally demonstrated it!

This is the same as having a clothing store and having a prospect see your ads, drive to your store, come in, and try on a pair of pants or a shirt.

As far as prospects go, you can't ask for any better.

These are the people you want to focus the majority of your marketing efforts on.

And the way you turn them into customers online is to use Multiple Conversion Points.

A conversion point is any point in your campaign where you ask for the order.

This can be your video sales letter, your webinar, your sales letter, your postcard ...whatever.

Most campaigns have only one conversion point.

More Conversion Points = More Money

I wanted more, so here's what I did.

I wrote a PDF sales letter outlining the offer I'd made at the end of the video.

The letter was thorough and detailed with a strong call to action.

Then I emailed it to just the people who'd completed the video ...but hadn't yet applied.

But that wasn't the end.

Behavioral Dynamic Response is THE pinnacle of Internet marketing and you should use it in everything you do.

So in this case, I tracked whether or not they clicked to download the PDF.

If they didn't download it, I had an email series that would remind them to go and read it.

But I went even further.

I made it so the PDF itself would only be available for a limited time ...and I let the prospect know when their access was expiring.

I was able to dynamically determine the expiration date and merge it into the emails they were getting so they'd say, "This letter is only available until Tuesday the 3rd" and so on ...with each user seeing a different date depending on when they'd finished the video.

The result was awesome!

95.89% of the people who watched the entire video responded to my email sequence about the PDF letter and downloaded it.

This is literally unheard of in Internet Marketing.

And is has nothing to do with the copy in the emails.

Instead, it's working because Behavioral Dynamic Response is being used to filter out who the most interested prospects are (those who finish the entire video) ...and then putting the most energy towards them.

Remember: Your sales are directly proportional to the amount of conversion points in your campaigns.

Then, I shifted my focus from "people who finished the video" to "people who also downloaded the PDF".

Also Remember - you always want to be analyzing your prospects' behavior and focusing all of your energy on the ones who demonstrate they're the most interested.

I created a three-part video series that literally showed them exactly what had happened to them each step of the way in the campaign they were in.

At the end of each video, I created another conversion point by asking them to apply for a consultation with my office.

And I used the same "countdown" techniques to get them to watch each new video as I'd used to get them to download the pdf.

Naturally, the majority of them watched the videos and I got even more applications.

The End Result.

First, and most importantly, this campaign created tons of goodwill with all the people who went through it.

They felt like they were receiving very valuable and helpful content ...not just a barrage of sales pitches.

This is critical because it increases our chances of getting new business from them later on.

Plus it helped build our brand and position us as a good company to deal with. (And it's just a great way to do business.)

The fortune really is in the follow up.

You can't bludgeon people with pitches and offers and expect it to work.

But if you have a truly Behaviorally Dynamic Campaign that tracks user behavior and responds accordingly ...you can see your sales grow like nothing before.

If you want something like that,

I've set aside some time for qualified buyers of this book to personally review your current sales and marketing process, and design a fully customized behavioral dynamic campaign for you ... FREE.

This is a genuinely free offer, and there are no strings attached.

In fact, it's even better than you realize.

Not only do we design the campaign for you, we also create a detailed blueprint of exactly how it works and give you that as well ...so you can deploy it immediately.

If that sounds interesting to you ...

Here's What To Do Next.

I've posted a short description of how this works here.
www.elitemarketingmachine.com/dynamic

It's simply a short letter that shows you what a typical blueprint and campaign diagram might look like, and walks you through exactly what will happen during your session.

This service is available to our Web Domination Clients at www.elitemarketingmachine.com/dynamic

"The Email Engine"

"The Email Engine" incorporates Behavioral Dynamic Response Marketing and is a detailed and completely automated email marketing system for all of your promotions and follow up campaigns.

We provide our Consulting Clients with up to 7 Customized fully automated Infusionsoft campaigns and over 30 tested and proven email series completely ready to implement into your business. Imagine having an automated money making Elite Marketing Machine.

The The Email Engine is perfect for any type or size of business. It doesn't matter the size or your email list, lack of a list, or if you're an established business looking to expand.

And Best of all… We do it all for you so you can focus on your business, family and passions.

5 Stages of The Email Engine

1. **Warm Up** – Introduce new prospects to your business or product, and turn strangers into friends.

2. **Involvement** – Talk to your prospects about what interests them and encourage them to buy your product or service.

3. **Sell Them Something Else** – Welcome your new customers or clients and encourage them to enhance or upgrade their experience by purchasing from you again.

4. **Segmentation** – Learn what your customers or clients want to learn more about and what they might want to buy next.

5. **Re-Involvement** – Bring prospects/Customers back when they've gotten out of touch or the relationship has been neglected.

Stage 1 - Warm Up

Great Job! You have a new prospect.

Someone signed up to receive your "Irresistible Incentive" called your office and left a message requesting more information, Downloaded a white paper or just gave you their card at an event.

Whatever the method: You have a new prospect on your email list.

What's the first thing you do with a new prospect?

First, they are more interested and eager to hear from you at this moment than they will ever be. Do things right, and you'll be a friend forever. Waste it, and you'll be seen as a nuisance and your e-mails will be marked as spam.

What to do:

• Introduce yourself and/or your Company

• Set expectations for what they will receive from you and how often.

• Restate the benefits of being a subscriber or prospect

• Get them to make micro-commitments

• Provide Curiosity (so they eagerly await your next e-mail).

If you design this first Warm Up email (the Welcome Email) correctly, you'll be much more likely to convert this lead into a customer.

A new lead must be **Warmed Up** to you and/or your business before they will interact. They must **Involve** themselves with you before they will buy; they must buy from you before they'll **Buy Something Else**; and once the process is over they will need to be **Segmented** based on their interest(s) before they become **Re-Involved** and buy from you again.

This is a proven system, and if you leave out one small piece of the system, the entire System falls apart.

To create a real "Email Engine"—you need to understand and use all 5 stages. You must also know how to move your prospects effortlessly from one stage to the next.

The first step is to educate your new prospect about you, your business or your product. You need to indoctrinate them.

- Who are you or What is your business?
- What are you about?
- Why are you different from everyone else?
- What should they expect from you?
- What should they do next?

Stage 2 - Involvement

The purpose of an Involvement email is to convert leads into customers.

When you have a new prospect, and they are fully warmed up to you and your business or product. And they are following you on social media, looking forward to and actually opening your emails...

It's time to make a sale.

But you can't rush. If you move too fast, you'll scare them off. It's like asking someone to meet your parents on a first date. It doesn't mean the person won't want to meet them at some point, but when you ask on the first date you just look like a weirdo, and the chances of that date ending immediately are pretty high.

How do you transition into a sale? Simple: You discuss whatever brought them to you in the first place.

The goal of an Involvement email series is to make that first sale to the person that has shown interest in something you have.

They've been segmented by opting in with their email address to get your Irresistible Incentive and will now start receiving an email series designed to sell them a product or service that corresponds with that interest.

"Irresistible Incentives" are important because they are the beginning of your Involvement Series. The quality of your Irresistible Incentive is critical to how quickly you will grow your list and if someone will even opt in to any particular Involvement Series to receive your offer.

A Irresistible Incentive is an easily consumable piece of content that solves a specific problem in a specific market that is offered in exchange for giving you their email.

For example it could be a 1 page PDF entitled:

5 Secrets to Eliminate Arthritis Pain That Doctors Will Never Tell You. This is just one of mine for my product Pain Relief Miracle

Stage 3 - Sell Them Something Else

This is where the majority of your money will be made.

For every offer you make to your clientele, there is a percentage of people that want to buy more from you. And that's why every buyer you get through an Involvement email series should receive an "upsell" to whatever you are selling. Leading them to another order.

When the Email Engine is working by turning cold leads into interested prospects and then into customers, it will also turn a portion of those buyers into repeat buyers, and that is where your real money will be made.

Assuming what you're offering is valuable, you'll find that once you get the first sale, it's much easier to make future sales to them. It is much easier and cheaper, in terms of advertising dollars and trust, to sell to a current customer than it is to find and sell to a new one.

When you have great products or services and combine that with a perfectly executed Email Machine Series, your customers have a better experience and your business reaps the financial rewards.

Here are examples of "Something Else To Sell"...

- **One-Time-Offer UpSell** – Offering a buyer more of what they just purchased. Ex. 4 more Bottles for 50% off

- **Cross-Sell** – A related end result to the first purchase. A one-hour consulting session to go along with the course they just bought.

- **Bundle Your Product or Service** – Multiple products in a package to create a new or better value. We offer 2 more bottles of PRM with a PRM Lotion a Roll on applicator and an Arthritis soak at a different price point different that if they purchased those separately.

- **Affiliate Offers** – Offer someone else's similar or related product as an affiliate to earn a commission from the sale. At the time of this writing there is a company selling $50,000 A DAY in an online weight loss Program offering a 75% commission on a $47 monthly recurring program.

- **Subscription or Membership Program** – Offer a product or service with recurring billing. After their initial purchase The PRM Preferred Customer program is a recurring $40 a month plan plus $6.95 shipping and customers receive a 1 month supply of PRM for $20 less than the initial price.

Stage 4 – Segmentation

The goal of the Segmentation Series is to get your prospect to show interest in whatever you are offering by opening, clicking or opting in to your offer. When they do, the prospect will be added to the appropriate email series.

Stage 5 Re-Involvement

When customers or leads stop opening your emails, you are leaving money on the table because your potential buyers aren't engaged.

A Re-Involvement Series is designed with your previous customers. If they were interested once, most likely they'll be interested again.

You just have present them something that will re-interest them in what you have to offer.

Some of my clients tell me that their customers are different... They say, "They don't want to hear from me after they buy my product."

Until I share the following story with them...

An Unexpected Lesson in Follow-Up

In most places the government regulates power company operations. What that means is that you don't have a choice who you buy electricity from, you have to buy it from the company that has facilities in your area. They are referred to as "regulated monopolies".

This means that no matter how upset you get with the power company, you have to either buy electricity from them or not have any... Let's face it, there are usually only two instances where you even think about the power company, when you get your bill each month and when the lights go out. Neither one is what you would call a positive experience.

In 2003 there was one such company whose customer satisfaction scores were not horrible but they certainly were not great. Then disaster! They got slammed with two of the worst hurricane seasons on record. They had back-to-back-to-back hurricanes that left the majority of their customers with out power for weeks.

Then, because they had exhausted their $1 Billion Dollar Storm Re-Building fund (power companies can't get insurance on their power lines) they had to go to their customers and tell them that we would have to charge them 10-15% more each month to replenish the fund.

To add insult to injury, the cost of fuel went through the roof during this same time frame and they had to increase their bills another 30% within a few short months.

Needless to say they had to deliver bad news to these customers over and over again during an 18-month stretch from August of 2004 to February of 2006. They were dreading the day that the customer satisfaction ratings would come out for the company.

The Shocking Truth

When they received their customer satisfaction scores they were blown away, the scores had improved to an all time high!

It turns out that because they were communicating so regularly with their customers, that even though they were calling/emailing/faxing to give their customers bad news, the customer's perception of the quality of service actually went up!

As a result they developed a 12-point communication plan so that now they are touching base with each major account at least once a month. In the next year they actually won an award for being best in class for customer satisfaction. So much for "no news is good news!"

What does this have to do with your company? Everything!

If customers who don't have a choice who they buy a service from get a sense of high customer support from increased communications... How much more impactful do you think it can be for your business! From my experience it is substantial!

Just imagine how happy your customers will be when they receive a message from you that you are having a sale, offering a new service, a VIP program, prize give-a-ways, or just sharing a helpful tip on how to get more value out of your product of service. If it works for a big power company it will work for you!

Branding

Properly branding your new business is one of the most important steps you can take on your way to successfully marketing your Local Business. Establishing your brand will inform potential clients of what your business does and who you are. One of the most important elements of your brand is your logo. It is what will become the face of your company and what people will associate with you and your business. Having consistency across all the platforms and strategies we have discussed is essential to portray a congruent brand.

When you properly brand your business, you will be able to set yourself apart from your competitors. Your business is unique, and it should be branded as such. This will also allow you to reach your target audience more effectively and create marketing plans centered on your brand. When properly implemented, a successful marketing plan will help you reach your target audience. This means those who can truly benefit from your particular products and services will hear your message.

Branding your business will also help you create an emotional connection with clients. When you emotionally connect with your clients, you will create a way in which they can identify and connect with your business. This can be achieved through the use of a well-designed logo and marketing plan.

Your logo is what will identify your business; because of this the design should be something that is recognizable as your brand and identifies your business.

A well-established brand is also an effective way to create trust in your target market. If potential clients believe that you are a trustworthy business, they are more likely to purchase your products and services. A business that is properly branded will experience a greater response from their emails, advertisements, and newsletters. As more people become invested in your brand, they will be more confident in the products and services that you offer. This trust can then translate to an increased amount of website traffic and sales.

When you are creating your brand, you should focus on the long-term goals of your business. Your brand is not something that is only being created to serve a short-term goal. The brand that you build should be strong enough to last through expansions and time while remaining consistent. This is the long-term marketing technique that appeals to audiences now and in the future.

Your brand should be designed to enhance your business, while adding a sense of permanence and reliability to your business. Your brand is what will be used to identify you now and in the years to come; because of this, it should be something that will instill trust in the minds of your clients today and in the future.

Online Reputation Management

Many business owners fail to recognize how important their online reputation is. It can make the difference between increased sales and a dramatic drop. Just one negative comment or review is enough to damage your online reputation. Once your reputation takes a hit, you will likely see a decrease in website traffic and the amount of sales you would normally experience. Below you will find some ways in which you can monitor and manage your online reputation.

In order to see what potential clients see when they search for your business, simply perform a search as they would. This will show you what is being presented to searchers and what is being said about you and your business. Regularly monitoring your online reputation will ensure that if there is any negative content being published, you are aware of it. If you know what is being said about you online, you are in a better position to take control of the situation and manage how the content is viewed.

During your research, if you notice any negative post or comment that has been published regarding your business you should act quickly to minimize any negative effect it may have. One negative comment can be enough to cost you potential clients. No matter how hard we try as business owners, we have to realize that we cannot please everyone 100% of the time.

If you notice a negative post on any of your social media pages, you should address that comment immediately. The quicker you act to remedy the situation the less likely the unhappy customer will be to post any additional comments.

If you choose to ignore the comment and not reply, the individual may continue to post additional comments, which can have a dramatically negative effect on your online reputation. The key is to act quickly and do everything within your power to solve the problem.

Taking a proactive approach to your online reputation can provide you with valuable insight into the type of content being published about your business and brand. The more involved you are in the process the easier it will be to notice any newly published negative content.

Once you are aware of this content, the key is to act quickly and decisively. This will ensure that the negative content is taken care of and any further searches will present people with positive reviews and content.

There is nothing that can damage a business more than negative comments posted online. However, if you are proactive and continue to monitor your online reputation, you will be better prepared to deal with these situations as they occur.

Landing Pages That Converts Prospects Into Customers

It Must Be Easy to Understand

Your landing page must have a clear and easy to understand offer.

Keep The Landing Page Simple

Don't use flash or fancy graphics. They only distract your visitor.

"Call Out" The Target Market

Your prospect needs to know immediately that they found the right place and that your Landing Page is for them. Use a Headline to "Call Out" to get their attention.

Examples:

- Attention Doctors!
- For Golfers!
- Attention Small Business Owners:
- For women who want to grow their business…
- For Lawyers only…

Use a benefit-rich Headline with a "Big Promise!"
- Solve the problem that keeps them awake at night
- Give them the silver bullet
- Offer them THE solution to their biggest problem.
- Offer them the magic pill

Examples of "Big Promise!" Headlines:

- Doctors In Sweden Say There IS A Cure For Arthritis!

- How to Win Friends and Influence People

- Look Years Younger, Pounds Lighter In 10 Short Days!

- Now! Turn Your Mind Into A Mental Magnet That Automatically Draws Friends, Power, Love, Money Far Beyond Your Fondest Dreams Into Your Life OVERNIGHT!

- How To Learn Without Studying!

- How To Stay Young Till 90

- How The Beautiful People Get Rid Of Both Cellulite And Ordinary Fat Without Dieting!

- How To Give Your Child The Top Grades In School He Deserves!

- How To Buy Money... Cheap!

Tell Them Specifically What To Do

Tell them what you want them to do and more importantly, how to do it by using a Call to Action. For Example. "Here's what you need to do next - Enter your best email in the box below and click the big orange button"

Make It Easy To Share On Social Media

Add Social Sharing buttons such as Facebook and Twitter to your Landing page or for the content you are giving away after they opt-in to your list.

Use Visual Cues

Control where your visitor looks when they are on your page using design elements such as 3 red arrows that point to the email submission field or a woman looking toward the opt-in box.

Reduce Distractions

Reduce or eliminate unnecessary actions they can take on your page.

Reduce The Number Of Information Fields On Your Form

The Less information you ask for, the higher your conversion rates.

I usually use a double opt-in. First I get their email and then if needed I get their name or address etc

Fewer Fields = Higher Conversions

Terms of Service and other Legal Documents
You must include your required Terms of Service, a Privacy Policy and other legal documents and disclaimers on your Landing Page

Facebook and Google Require them.

Action buttons must Stand Out
Use a color that isn't used anywhere else on the page.

Put the action button "Above The Fold"
"Above The Fold" is when the button can be seen without them scrolling down the page to get to it.

Use Benefit Rich Wording Inside The Action Buttons
Reinforce the main benefits of your offer with text.

For Example:
Yes Jason! I Want More Customers!

This is known as a "Call To Action"

11 Essentials to Marketing Online

With the countless methods of promotion being enlisted in today's market, it is vital to make sure that your company stays in step. Marketing your business online takes planning, commitment and the decision to use the tools wisely.

Here are 11 Essentials to keep in mind as you begin:

Essential 1

Before you begin your campaign, take time to carefully plan a strategy. What is your goal? What do you plan to gain? How much time can the company devote to research and analysis? One surefire plan is to start with the basics and grow from there.

Essential 2

Make certain that your website and contact information on all web searches are kept current. Check all links and backlinks to make sure that they are validated and functioning. Remove any that aren't working to ensure that you get constant traffic, unhindered by bugs.

Essential 3

Treat your online plan and the maintenance as a legitimate department. Have 'department meetings' on a regular basis to appropriately monitor data and make needed adjustments. Assuming that automations and follow-ups will happen on their own will cause huge mistakes and could create missteps and missed opportunities.

Essential 4

Keep consistent in your contact. Make sure that the clients hear from you. Share the most pertinent information about your business and any important dates. Share your business success stories and new changes that may be on the horizon.

Essential 5

Make sure that your company's mission is always kept in the forefront. Test all content and other writings against it to ensure that they are aligned. Make sure that anyone you contract any of your marketing services to is also very aware of your mission. Have an approval process for content before it is allowed to be posted.

Essential 6

Use social media. Good news travels fast, but bad news travels faster. Make sure that the messages and social connection opportunities are a positive reflection of your business by finding clients who are willing to write positive reviews and comments on pages like Facebook and Google +.

Essential 7

Join a forum or a blog that is geared specifically toward an audience for your business. Create a niche and use it often. The more visible your company is, the more traffic you get and the greater your connections and earning potential can be.

Essential 8

Make sure that your clients have a venue available that allows them to give feedback and suggestions. They will feel heard and become loyal to your company and your brand.

Essential 9

Program any of your client contact systems to key in on special dates like customer birthdays, the anniversary of them first visiting your company. The options for specialization are many. This, too, will build greater confidence in your business.

Essential 10

Make sure that your entire staff is involved and that they share your mission with the same vigor and enthusiasm that you would; communication is key.

Essential 11

Don't let inactivity and outdated content destroy your hard work or your reputation. If it isn't relevant, delete it. Now you have the principles and techniques to quickly grow your business.

If you would like to expedite the Marketing process explained in this book you can visit www.EliteMarketingMachine.com and we will help you dominate your local market and establish you and your business as the expert in your area.

Elite Marketing Done-For-You Services

Mobile Apps

1. Be Visible to your Customers at All Times
Statistics show that the average American spends more than two hours a day on his or her mobile device.

2. Create a Direct Marketing Channel
Apps can provide general info, prices, booking forms, search features, user accounts, messengers, news feeds, and much more.

One of the biggest benefits of having a mobile app is that all the information you'd like to provide to your customers – including special sales and promotions – is right at their fingertips. Through push notifications you're getting even closer to a direct interaction, and can easily remind customers about your products and services whenever it makes sense.

3. Build Brand and Recognition
A mobile app for your business can greatly contribute to your brand awareness. I'd like to break this topic down into two aspects, the combination of which will make your app a true winner.

4. Improve Customer Involvement
No matter whether you are selling flowers or spa services, your customers need a way to reach you. Having a messaging (or help desk) feature within your app can really make a difference in the way you communicate with your customers.

5. Stand Out From the Competition
Mobile apps at the small business level are still rare, and this is where you can take a big leap ahead of your competitors.

6. Cultivate Customer Loyalty
Make a true and sincere connection with your customers.

Mobile Friendly Website Design

If you do not have a website, the question is not whether you need one, it's how fast we can build it! In today's world having a website is 100% necessary for 99% of all business owners.

Since all Internet Marketing efforts drive traffic to a website, having a quality site is central to marketing success.

- If you're just starting a business, a website needs to be part of your business plan.

- If you already have a website, it may need a redesign to leverage new technology, make it mobile responsive, or give it a fresh look that keeps up with the times.

Our Web Design Services include base packages that cover core client needs and add ons that do just about everything else.

Get exactly the site you need with a range of Add-Ons from design, content, support, performance, social, and more:

Local Web Domination Package

This is our **Elite Level Package.** It is guaranteed to establish you, your company, product or service across the Web to **Dominate Your Competition.** <u>It is only for the most serious business owner.</u> **You must apply for consideration** as we only work with ONE Business in each category per city.

Package Includes but NOT LIMITED TO:

Customized Done-For-You Services

Custom Marketing Plan with Dynamic Behavioral Response

Mobile Website and Mobile App Design and Hosting

Local Buzz services for your business

Brand Establisher - Business Directory, Setup and Submissions

Brand Booster - Boost Brand Awareness across the Web

Video creation, submission and optimization

Social Media Branding, Setup and Maintenance

Blog Setup and Maintenance

Monthly e-mail and Direct Mail Campaign Management

Automated Email Engine Integration

Facebook and Google Adwords Campaign Management

Online Reputation Management

Cosmetic Surgeon Case Study: The $37,214 email

Before Local Web Domination:

Cosmetic Surgeon - $517,000 Previous 12 Months Revenue

2,000 client email list that was never mailed

Email Campaign #1

"Botox Special" - Sold out of 1000 units of Botox. Office sold other services to clients when they came in to the practice.

First email $37,214 in extra sales in 24 hours

Direct Mail Campaign -"Skin Tightening Treatment"

3 new customers per month =	**$9,000/month**
$1,500 Free Cruise for Most Referrals	$100,000 extra revenue

Results:

1 email offer per month =	$20,000/Month
1 Direct Mail Offer per month =	$9,000/Month
	$348,000/Year

Total Web Domination	**$212,000 in sales**

12 Months After Implementation	**$1,214,000**

Custom Sales Funnel Design

Opt In Funnel Design and Implementation

A Done-For-You opt in funnel with custom email follow-up templates. Designed to grow your customer base and increase sales both online and "in-store".

Fully Integrated Sales Funnel

This is a fully Done-For-You, Automated Sales funnel.
Includes custom email follow up templates and reporting.

Local Buzz

Optimization of local listings, maps, reviews, & check-in promos can help customers find you before they find your competitors?

Local listings are increasingly used by people who are searching for products and services in their vicinity, who are also ready to make purchases either online or offline.

Local Places Research
Duplicate Google Places Analysis

Duplicated listings for a single business can be problematic when they appear in Google search results or in a business owner's Google Places account. There should only be one listing per business location, both in the Google Places account and in search results. We will develop the best solution should your business appear more than once in your account or in search results. We will present the proposed changes before implementing any modifications.

Duplicate Foursquare Analysis

Foursquare is one of many secondary local search engines where you will need to list/claim and verify your business. Listing and claiming your business properly with Foursquare is an essential step to improving your local presence.

One can't create duplicate listings in Foursquare. If there's an existing listing, we will report it to you so you can decide if you would like us to claim it. Otherwise, should Foursquare creation be part of your package, we will create and optimize a new listing for you.

Duplicate Facebook Places Analysis

Facebook allows people to share where they've been, where they're headed and where they are now. This feature is an opportunity for businesses to promote their products and services within their local area.

We will find duplicate Places for your business by searching for its name or locations where people made when they checked in. If we found duplicates, we will claim and merge the duplicates to keep your customers' likes and check-ins in one place.

Duplicate Bing Local Analysis

Having your business added properly in Bing Business Portal is an important step in improving your local presence. Bing is one of the major search engines where you can have your business listed and verified.

We will find duplicate listings in Bing by searching for its name or locations and report it to Bing if we find any duplicates.

Competition Category Analysis

We conduct Competition Category Analysis to see how you're performing and to acquaint you with the existing competition for your category. We will then compare our analysis with that of other advertisers in your niche/category. With this data, we can make informed decisions on which types of optimization changes are suitable for your account. This is important because "categories" in Google places are not selected from a drop down menu, they are typed in. Therefore the options of what to enter as a category are limitless.

Ranking Comparison Report - Google, Yahoo, Bing

This service triangulates search results gathered from leading search engines. We will analyze your business website's rankings based on their positions on these search engines in relation to your chosen search terms. The comparison is made by looking for your details on the three largest search engines today (Google, Yahoo!, and Bing). Local search results (Google Places, Yahoo! Local, and Bing Local) will also be part of the report and shown side by side of your organic rankings.

Current Directory Listing Analysis and Overview

We will be running a report to analyze your current Local Directory Standings:

What business directories is your business currently listed in? What type of information is the directory submission site using? Is your listing using a description or photos? Does your listing currently contain any reviews or have a star rating?

Local Online Directories are the modern equivalent of the Yellow Pages. As more local consumers turn to the Internet to find information about Local Businesses, these directories are seeing a huge growth in users. Directories can be a direct source of new customers but they can also boost your local SEO ranking. Therefore it's important that your business is listed on all these leading directories and that your business information on them is correct.

Business Address Consistency Check among Existing Directories

It's important for your Business Name, Address, and Phone Number to be recorded consistently across all the main search engines and local directories. Inaccurate information can be confusing for customers and more so for Google. Google likes to verify the information it holds about your business with other sources such as local online directories.

It is ideal that your Name, Address, and Phone Number are the same on each site. If there are any discrepancies, appropriate measures should be implemented. Updating the inaccurate results by claiming your listing on those directories and correcting the erroneous information effectively resolves this issue.

Google Places Competition Profile Page Analysis

This process efficiently analyzes your performance on Google Places. Google Places is Google's local search service and contains listings of Local Businesses, organizations, and places. Google often shows Google Places results for search queries that contain a location (also known as a Geotag). It is also used in Google's local applications for mobile phones. Google Places is a very powerful Local Marketing tool and should be utilized by all Local Businesses.

This research compares your Google Places listing to your top 5 Google competitors.

These competitors are the top ranked companies for your target search terms. We will be analyzing your competitors quantity of photos, reviews, videos, star rating and other factors such as their categories, description, and verification status.

Local On-Page Optimization Analysis

This section analyzes the On-Site SEO factors that affect your ability to rank high in search engines and specifically the Google Places/ Maps. On-Site SEO factors comprise the fundamental elements on your website, either visible on the page (which you can readily see) or seen only in your website's code (which search engines scout for). It's easier to improve SEO factors on your own site because you have control over them. Listed below is a quick bullet list of some of the components we will be analyzing:

- Meta Tags and Page Titles
- Heading Tags
- Robots.txt
- Error Pages
- Keyword Visibility per Target Page
- Primary Location Visibility Check on Website
- Internal Site linking structure
- Sitemap
- Contact Us Page Analysis
- Microformat Analysis

Google Places Compatibility Check

This section analyzes your performance in Google Places. We will examine your website's categories, rank, verification status, number of reviews, and Google's star rating. We will also pay close attention to your current listing if it includes any type of coupon promotions. In doing so, we are able to quickly analyze the flaws in the current Google Local Listing. Should one exist, we will immediately determine if it matches your company name, phone number, and address.

Business Information Intake

This form is provided to gather all the necessary information to facilitate the optimization process and should be filled out in full and returned so we may proceed with the optimization process.

Business Information Validation

It is very important that all company information on the Internet is consistent with your website. We will use the pieces of information on the form and verify them against the target website and any other directories we can find online. We do this to ensure that the information we are using is updated. This also guarantees that all information about your business on the Internet is consistent.

Business Address Verification (if applicable)

We check to make sure the address given for the business location matches a verified location in the USPS official database. It is not confirmed but heavily believed that Google cross references the USPS official database to check the validity of the business location. We will be able to tell if the address is residential or commercial. Note this is only for USA clients.

Uploading of Logo for Linking into Local Listings

In order to upload a Logo to a Local Business Listing, the logo must first be hosted online and assigned a corresponding URL.

Google Places - Creation and Optimization

Our Google Local services includes the creation, optimization and submission of a Google Local Business Listing. The listing must be claimed by receiving a PIN number. This PIN number will be sent to you within 2 weeks of us making the request. Once you receive the PIN number on the post card, you will need to email it to us so we can claim the listing for you.

Google Plus User Account Creation

If a Google Plus User account and its password are not provided once the campaign launches, we will create a Google Plus User account for you. This is required for us to create your Google Plus Business Page.

Google Plus Business Page Creation

Your Google Plus Business page is your brand's home on Google. When your customers search on Google, the results may include relevant posts, photos, and videos from your Google+ page. Get found across Google, right when your customers are most interested.

We will create and optimize this page for your company to have maximum exposure in Google Plus. We will help you stand out from the competition by including compelling online content such as photos and logos. We will also add your business hours, services, and other information.

Bing Local - Creation and Optimization

Our Bing Local services include the creation, optimization and submission of the Bing Business Portal. We will help you stand out from the competition by including compelling online content such as photos and logos. We will also add your business hours, services and other information. It typically takes two to three weeks for a Bing Local listing to be published.

If your business is located outside of the US, we will be creating a Yelp listing instead since the Bing Business portal is not available in your location. As with Bing, it will typically take two to three weeks for your Yelp listing to be published.

Facebook Places - Creation and Optimization

We will set up a Facebook Places Page on your behalf. People can check into this Page when they're nearby. We will make sure that your Facebook page contains accurate information. We will add your company description, phone number, location, hours of operation, specialties, services, payment options, etc. Facebook Places requires phone verification.

Foursquare - Creation and Optimization

Claiming and verifying your listing in Foursquare is the first step to get discovered and be successful in Foursquare. Foursquare has millions of business listings, all submitted by customers who go to those places.

We will find your business and make sure that the information for your claimed business is accurate. We will add your company description, phone number, hours of operation as well as links to your website and social media profiles – Facebook, Twitter, etc.

Verification of Foursquare will require a credit card payment of $1.

Additional Top Local Business Directories

Top Local Directory Account Creation and Optimization

While setting up your listings in Primary Local Business Directories, we will also submit your business information to top local directories such as Yelp, Judysbook, and Insiderpages. As more and more local consumers turn to the Internet to find information about Local Businesses, these citation directories are witnessing a huge growth in popularity. These citation directories can be a direct source of new customers, but they can also boost your local presence.

Top Niche or Geo Related Directory Account Creation and Optimization

We will conduct a research to find niche specific or geo related directories. Using this data we will be able to not only target the directories that is niche specific or geo targeted for better local presence, but we will be also able to find directories where your target market hangs out. Our ability to use specialized research and citation/directory tracking resources will give us a leg up on your competition.

Image Creation, Optimization, and Publication

High Quality Image Sourcing

We will find compelling, high quality, relevant images to represent your brand. Finding the right image is crucial in increasing your sales, market share and brand recognition.

Image Optimization and Publication

We will optimize the branded images without changing their look or visual quality. These images will load fast which increases the likelihood of being exposed to consumers in the world wide web. Images will have the ability to index in the search engines when your clients type in relevant keywords describing your business. Images are often times part of the first page search engines results.

Image Geotagging and Backlink Generation

After uploading your branded images online, we will write optimized descriptions and insert BB Codes to generate backlinks pointing to your website. We will also geotag these images to help improve your local presence and pin point the images location on a map.

Image Uploading/Publishing in Major Local Business Directories

Branded images will be also uploaded to the primary 4 Local Business directories in a form of an update. This will help in increasing brand awareness which could later lead to sales and conversions.

Misc. Service Items
Dedicated IP Services

We will provide a dedicated IP for each campaign for use when accessing your accounts.

Reporting and Auditing
Internal Report Auditing and Analysis

All Reporting is subjected to a monthly routine auditing and assessment process. We perform this auditing on a monthly basis to assure that all reports are up to date, error free and properly formatted.

Directory Research

You may choose between Blog and Forum Comment Posting AND Review Publication

For the Blog and Forum Comment Posting: we will conduct research to find blogs and forums that are relevant to your business, and perform posting of relevant comments with reference to your business.

For the Review Publication: Upon being furnished with reviews you have collected, we will publish each of them to one of the top review publication websites.

Specialized Directory Creation

Collectively, Local Online Citation Directories are the modern equivalent of the Yellow Pages. As more and more local consumers turn to the Internet to find information about Local Businesses, these citation directories are witnessing a huge growth in popularity. These citation directories can be a direct source of new customers, but they can also boost your local places rankings.

The directories we decide to built new listings in will be determined by the "Directory Research" as described in the above line item. Another way to gain prominence on these citation directories is to enhance your listing with more detail about your business.

We will create directory listings using (limited to) the below information.

*Company Name
*Website
*Address
*Local Phone Number
*Services
*Categories
*Email Address
*Products and Brands
*Logo

Blog and Forum Comment Posting OR Review Publication

You may choose between Blog and Forum Comment Posting AND Review Publication

For the Blog and Forum Comment Posting: we will conduct research to find blogs and forums that are relevant to your business, and perform posting of relevant comments with reference to your business.

For the Review Publication: Upon being furnished with reviews you have collected, we will publish each of them to one of the top review publication websites.

Content

Page Content (Data entry)
Want to update your site? You can add content through the WordPress Content Management System, using an already existing page layout. This includes things like adding blog posts, pdf's, images, and new pages in the navigation (provided that we copy an existing page's layout).

Page Template

We can create a new page layout. This is for adding in a page with a completely new / different layout from all the other pages. You will be able to use this new page layout to add in more content in the future using the WordPress dashboard.

Product entry (e-commerce must exist)

We can populate your e-commerce system with your product offerings. If you just don't have the time to put in those hundreds of products, let us do it for you.

Image/file upload and integration
We can upload and integrate all sorts of files into your website. Do you have PDF catalogs? Images for your gallery or portfolio? We'll put them all in for you!

Advanced

eCommerce

Generate Revenue directly from your site! Sell and take payments online! We can create an e-commerce site that will enable you to generate overflowing cash revenue. Just ask your web design consultant so we can cost it out properly for you.

Membership

Do you want your site viewers to be able to register or login to you site? Are you giving them access to specific service areas or products that only members can avail of? Do you want to track their information or details? Do you want them to be able to submit information or files to the site? All of this and more can be done - kindly speak to your web design consultant so we can cost it out properly for you.

Testimonial Function

Testimonials are a great way to show potential customers how happy you can make them. Get viewers to put in their own testimonials. Screen your testimonials to make sure you don't get any unwanted spam or bot messages.

Gallery Function

Do you have a lot of photos? Categories and organize them in albums, put up an online gallery where your customers can peruse through your photos with ease.

Custom Post-Type

A custom post-type is a special type of page / post which a specific set of fields. Normally, you will be able to put in a Title, and Content into your site.

With a custom post-type, we can create a specific set of fields which will allow you to easily put in content into your site that matches a certain look and layout.

You can for example have fields for a recipe, or a business, and these will show up in an organized way without having to do a single word of code.

PayPal Checkout Button

We can embed a PayPal checkout button on your site for you. This is ideal if you are only selling one product. Simply give us the code that is generated by PayPal for you and we'll integrate it into your site.

Directory Listing

A directory listing system will allow site members to put in details about their businesses. Create an online directory and charge your business partners for giving them leads and customers. Be a central hub by giving your site viewers access to the different business partners that you have.

Advanced Form Creation

For complex forms that allows for conditional fields that can also be easily integrated with a variety of third party services i.e., Infusionsoft, Mailchimp, Aweber, PayPal, Constant Contact, Freshbooks, and many more.

Automated Language Translator

Instantly translate to Spanish "Ola!", French "bonjour", German "Guten Tag", and many more using Google's language translator.

Alternative Language Input

Have a multilingual site with an accurate language variant. Translate to Spanish, French, German, Italian and many more without worrying on grammatical errors or missed translations.

Social Media Login for Comments

Allow your visitors to comment, login and register with Social Networks i.e., Facebook, Twitter, Google, LinkedIn, Instagram, Yahoo, etc...

BuddyPress

A social network in a box! BuddyPress allows users to make connection, profiles, message posting, and interact in groups. It enables you to build a community for your company, school, or any niche community.

Forum System

Start conversations and ask questions! Post a topic that you can moderate!

Events Management / Booking and Reservation
Ad Management

Real Estate Listings

Are you selling property? Leasing apartments? Renting out commercial space? This is just the thing for you. Put up your properties online, put in the details, then start marketing them to your clients.

Design

Banner

We can design graphic banners for your website homepage. Do you have new promo or a new service? Let your customers know with a nifty new banner image!

Button

Do you want a specific kind of button or icon that you just can find? Have us make it for you!

HTML Page

We can create a hard-coded HTML page, instead of utilizing a Content Management System. This is useful if you want something up very quickly and with static content that will not change. Useful for promos or landing pages which you will be taking down after a certain date.

Mockup

Do you just want a mockup? Do you want to see what your site will look like first before we start building it? Have us make one for you!

Logo

Everything starts with your business identity. You don't have one? Start with a logo! Check out some samples of our high-end logo design services: www.services.elitemarketingmachine.com/portfolio

Popular

Rush Service
Need your site build yesterday? If it's important enough to you we'll put extra resources on your project and push it out by a fixed date from when you've provided the required data and digital assets.

General Plugin Install (no configuration or setup)
Have a plugin you want to install? Let us do it for you. We'll check if there's any conflict with existing plugins, and we'll do some basic setup to make sure it works. For large complex plugins that require configurations however, we won't actually configure it for you, such plugins usually have extended functionality that have their own costs (kindly see the "extended add-on" section).

Landing Page
A stand-alone page in a WordPress site with a unique layout design specifically for a certain function. Drive your PPC campaigns or marketing efforts to this landing page to get more conversions. Design a solid user experience which will convert your traffic into sales or leads. You can select from our various landing page templatges from; http://marketinghelper.net/pay-per-click/

WordPress Blog Install
WordPress Security Lockdown

Blog setup (on existing WordPress Site)

Setup a blog on an already existing WordPress site - utilize dynamic content to give you site more credibility.

Site Migration

If you already have a site and you just want to move it to a different hosting provider, then rest easy and just have us do it for you.

Extra revision round

Our website design package come with a default of 2 revision rounds. Sometimes though, especially if you are unsure about the direction you want to move forward with, you may find that you need an additional round of revisions.

3-month Backup and Storage

It's always a good idea to backup your site. If anything goes wrong, rest assured that we have backups in our system and all your hard work was not lost.

Cross-browser compatibility

If you are using an external theme, we can do cross-browser checks to make sure that it will work well for all updated browsers. This already comes with your package if you go with the Premium Themed package and above.

Analytics and Webmasters Installation

Measure your site performance! You need data and information to find out how your site is doing, we can help with that by Installing and registering Google Webmasters and Analytics for your site domain.

Support & Maintenance

Quarterly Website Maintenance

Get up to 4 hours of support every month per quarter! We have completely separate ticketing system which will allow you to give us tasks to update and maintain your site. quick turnaround times, and direct support. If you regularly want to do changes to your site, or put in more content, then this is just the service that you need.

Semiannual Website Maintenance

Get up to 4 hours of Web design support every month, for six months. Perfect for all those small jobs essential to keeping a site fresh, like adding content, WordPress updates, logo change, etc. Plus a 24 hour response time guaranteed!

Annual Website Maintenance

Get up to 4 hours of Web design support every month, for 12 months. Perfect for all those small jobs essential to keeping a site fresh, like adding content, WordPress updates, logo change, etc. Plus a 24 hour response time guaranteed!

Additional 4 hours for Quarterly/Annual Package

If you need additional support hours beyond what was paid for in your Quarterly or Annual Package, you can buy them in 4 hour buckets. Must already have purchased the Quarterly or Annual Package.

Minimum Recommended

Social Media Feed

Make your site dynamic! A widget area can be configured so that you will have a feed (updates) from your Facebook or twitter account directly on your site. This is useful for lending credibility to your site by utilizing social media. Especially if you have a Social Media Campaign running with us.

Speed Optimization

A fast site is a good site. Customers will usually not wait around if your site takes too long to load. We will build and optimize your site load time to make sure it passes Google Page Speed tests. Reduce your bounce rate by making sure your site pages load quickly.

Lead Capture

The heart and soul of any website - make sure that your website isn't just an online brochure. Capture leads for potential customers and give them free offers. Turn your traffic into revenue!

Speed Optimization

A fast site is a good site. Customers will usually not wait around if your site takes too long to load. We will build and optimize your site load time to make sure it passes Google Page Speed tests. Reduce your bounce rate by making sure your site pages load quickly.

All Recommended

Do you want a fast loading website with the ability to receive social media feeds and capture leads to potential customers? Our recommended add-ons are there for a reason; these make the difference between a good website and a great website. Get them all at a discounted price. Save 20% if you get them all!

Website SEO Services

Search engine optimization is the process of improving the ranking of your web pages on search engines' organic or unpaid search results pages (such as Google, Yahoo and Bing) for search queries related to your business, brand, product or service against your competition. And because of this, SEO will give you high visibility and ranking and so giving you more traffic to your website and a higher chance of getting leads, conversions and sales for your business.

Recommended Minimum Duration

The minimum recommended duration for any SEO marketing campaign is 12 months. Ideally SEO campaigns run forever. SEO marketing is a long term marketing strategy that should be factored into a company's monthly overhead. The minimum duration is stated to give a milestone as to when you should be able to see satisfactory to ideal ranking and traffic results.

Keep in mind there are many other factors that determine ranking and traffic outcome as a result of a SEO marketing campaign. What is contained within this proposal does not cover 100% of ranking and traffic factors. We recommend you to run this marketing campaign for a minimum of one year, with a thorough check-in analysis every 6 months.

Number of Primary Keywords

Primary keywords are the keywords we consider to be the highest priority. Typical marketing campaigns have "keyword groups". Each primary keyword should have 2 related secondary keywords. Within one keyword group, the primary keyword would be the most competitive, and the two related "secondary keywords" would be less competitive. We recommend keyword grouping in this manner to help structure our content siloing.

Number of Secondary Keywords

Secondary keywords are related to a specific primary keyword. Each primary keyword will have two related secondary keywords, which are less competitive. Target keywords are grouped together and each keyword in a keyword group has a different competition level. Typically, one keyword will stand out with the most competition. The main benefit in grouping keywords together in the manner of 1 primary to 2 secondary, is the ability to put more effort and energy into the primary keywords.

One primary keyword could have MUCH more value and traffic than a secondary keyword, and therefore, it is of extreme importance for us to classify and group the target keywords accordingly.

Manual and Software Driven Keyword Research

Manual Keyword Mining

Before launching a marketing campaign we need to know what keywords to target. A "keyword" is what we refer to as the word or phrased typed into a search engine to return search results. Utilizing software and several man hours of filtering through the Google data, we return a full keyword report. The report not only shows keyword traffic, but also competition analysis and where the website is currently ranking in Google, Yahoo, and Bing for that particular keyword. The keywords chosen determine the direction of the entire marketing campaign, thus the extreme importance we place on keyword research.

Keyword Ranking Report

Keyword Rankings, or where your site is ranked in search engines for keywords, has a major impact on your Web traffic, lead generation and conversions. Research shows more than 75% of all search engine users click on a result on the first page; so the higher you rank in the search engine results pages, the better your chances are of gaining more traffic.

Using specialized software, the rankings of the target keywords for the website will be generated and tabulated. The results will be used as a reference point for the initial rankings of the keywords before the marketing campaign is commenced.

Keyword Competition Analysis

We analyze the competitors for every keyword you want to target. It is important for us to look at the competition to have a better understanding of the keyword competition level.

Keyword Grouping

This is where we group the target keywords that have been agreed upon into sets of 1-3 keywords which will then be designated to target pages during the URL Mapping stage. Keywords of a given campaign are grouped based on, but not limited to, similar keywords, related terms, and geo-target.

URL Architecting

By organizing the URLs, it will also helps organize the entire website. By having a proper URL structure, it will help users to easily determine what page they are on by just looking at the URL alone. Most websites do not have a proper url structure and simple put all pages as a direct extension off the homepage.

The search engines can only interpret a website as well as it is built. Having properly structured URLs is essential to ensure maximum rankability of your website.

URL Mapping

If an SEO campaign has 30 keywords, they will not all go on the same page. We usually target 1 keyword on each page, with unique exceptions to the homepage. The process of determining which page should contain certain keywords is URL mapping.

Factors such as theme relevance and page rankings will come into play when URL mapping is performed. Among the target pages that are prioritized are those that are convertible and/or will catch a user's attention, engaging them and encouraging them to interact and browse through the site. The homepage, which is the most highly evaluated page among all the others, is always targeted. If a page with a matching theme does not exist for certain keywords, then a new page with fresh content will have to be created.

Target URLs

The Target URLs are determined during keyword URL mapping. These URLs are simply the pages we are primarily targeting with our On Page and Off Page optimizations. When we track the keyword rankings, these are the pages you should see rankings respective to the keywords targeted on each page.

10 Major Business Directories Setup

We will set up and optimize the 10 major business directories for you. Online business directories have taken over the stereotypical "Yellow Pages," and it is a must for all business owners to at least have a presence in the top 10 business directories online. We will create your business directory accounts and make sure they are filled out and well optimized.

The business directories we will set up include but are not limited to:

Yahoo and Bing Local
Manta
Super Pages
Yelp
MapQuest Local
HotFrog
Angie's List
Kudzu
Yellow Pages
Metrobot

Note: These directories will vary based on your country and also the current priority status for the respective directory.

5 Major Press Release Accounts Setup

When we write press releases we need a way to publish those press releases to the world. Although we do this through your social channels, we also want to be able to get these press releases published on official press release websites. The benefit of publishing the press release on an official press release website is the exposure. Searchers can go on the press release websites, find your press release, share it with their friends, like it with Facebook, +1 it with Google plus, and even link to it in other conversations.

We will be creating your accounts in the top 5 free press release publication sites during the first month of the marketing campaign.

The list of press release sites we will set up include but are not limited to:

PRLog.org
PR.com
PR-Inside.com
I-Newswire.com
OnlinePRNews.com

Google + Account Creation - Authorship Account

If you do not have a Google + account setup, we will create an account for you. The Google + account we would setup (or be given from you) will need to have a user that we can use an the "Author" for blog articles. For instance, if you has a Google + account that you want us to use but you do not want to be visible on your blog or in the search engines as an Author, then you should give us a different account that you would be ok with us using as an author. Some companies choose to create a "dummy" user as their author so they can use it universally and also so that their content is not marked as "authored" by an employee that could leave the company.

What else do we use a Google + account for? The Google + access is the same access as Gmail, so make sure that if you hand us over a Google + account to manage that you are ok with us having the Gmail access because it is the same thing. If you are not ok with us having Gmail access then please make sure to provide a different account or allow us to create one for you. We will use the same Google + access to also setup the blogger, YouTube and other related Google accounts.

Google + Business Page Setup

The Google + business page will be setup as a page off of your Google + account. The business page is like having your own mini business website on your Google +. Business pages are important for social networking, SEO, claiming publisher ownership over your website content, and it allows your clients/customers to "Check In" using their Google latitude phone app. We will complete the business page for you and make sure it is optimized and updated with the content we create on a monthly basis.

10 Major Social Media Accounts Setup

We will set up your 10 major social media accounts for you. For SEO, reputation management, and raw traffic generation value, it is important for you to have set up and maintained your top 10 social media accounts. Social media accounts help to establish your brand, and it will help us to associate your brand to your website. Your social media accounts will also be used for content publication, generating back links, and attracting more visitors to your website.

The social media accounts generated could include but are not limited to:

Facebook

NewsVine

Twitter

AOL Lifestream

LinkedIn

Plurk

Google Plus

Friend Feed

App.net

Feedspot

10 Major Social Sharing Accounts Setup

We will set up your 10 major social sharing accounts for you. Social sharing websites are specifically created for sharing content and making your sharing decisions publicly available. Your social sharing accounts will help us to build back links to your website, and they will help us to tell the world about the new content we will be generating for you on a monthly basis.

The Social Sharing Accounts established could include but are not limited to:

Bitly

InstaPaper

Delicious

Slashdot

StumbleUpon

Bibsonomy

Diigo

Pocket

Folkd

Storify

5 Major Off-site Blog Accounts Setup

Off-Site blogs are extremely important in today's online marketing world. Of course, having great written content on your website is of the highest priority, but having multiple blogs with a significant amount of authority can really boost your rankings. One of the best things about having your own off-site blogs is the ability to have full control. When we set up the blogs, we will have the ability to control comments and what is published.

The off-site blog will be used to publish content, establish brand, and build back links.

The list of off-site blogs we setup include but are not limited to:

Blogger
Wordpress
Tumblr
LiveJournal
Scoop.it

Google + Publisher Setup

Have you ever wondered how Google knows if you own the content on your website? Google has incredibly complex algorithms to determine the uniqueness factor of the content on your website. Since content originality is so important to Google, it is important to claim ownership of the content on your website through Google's eyes. Now you can! We can create a business page on your Google+ account and generate a unique tag from your business page to install on your website. This tag will tell Google that your Google+ business is the publisher of the content on your website. In other words, you are telling Google you are the publisher of the content on your website.

Blog Category Setup

Regardless of whether you have an existing WordPress blog on your website, or if we have to set up one for you, we still need to configure your blog. Establishing the categories on a blog is very important. When you go into a blog and all you see are archive dates to old blog posts, you have no way to easily navigate to the type of content you are looking for. That would be the equivalent of going to a website with no main navigation. Hence, it is very important for us to establish categories in your blog.

For blogs that do not have very many relevant articles, we highly recommend adding a category for "Previous Publications" and adding all that old content you have onto the blog.

The standard universal blog categories are:

Company Updates

Press Releases

Promotions

General Information

Previous Publications (for old content in your closet)

Uploading of Provided Blog Articles (from you)

During the first month of the campaign we ask you to gather all the old content you can find that is related to your business. Most companies have a tremendous amount of written content stored in old file cabinets; from research to old promotions. Having relevant content on your website is extremely important and most websites struggle to have a significant amount of relevant content published on their website.

We will create a category on your blog called "Previous Publications". The blog category is intended solely for old content that might be out-dated. Content published in this category must be relative to the business's services or products, however being outdated is of no concern because the blog category lets searchers know that the content in this category is consider a previous publication and might be out dated.

Just like a Facebook timeline, old events or publications are still relevant to users, and having this additional content will help the website to rank better for your target keywords.

To motivate you to dig through your closet, old file cabinets, and your computers in a effort to find great content to publish, we are offering to upload X amount of content to your blog free of charge. We want to make the most of your marketing campaign and as the company owner you have the highest authority on your business and your previously written content could be of extreme value in our marketing campaign.

Domain Redirect Optimization

Domain Redirect Analysis

Some websites use both the WWW and the non-WWW version of its URLs. If this is the case, and the site does not redirect to WWW if non-WWW is used and vice versa, then the site needs to be redirected to its appropriate URL. Here, we will be determining which version should be used for your site in the search results so that the rankings and traffic will not be distributed and search engines will not interpret them as duplicates or different pages (http://www.google.com/support/webmasters/bin/answer.py?answer=44231).

Domain Redirecting

If necessary and given the appropriate access, we will be implementing the 301 domain redirect to our recommended version - either WWW or non-WWW.

Homepage Redirect Optimization

Homepage Redirect Analysis

Similar to the Domain Redirect Analysis, we will be checking if the homepage has different URL versions and determining which version should be used for your site in the search results.

Examples:
Example.com, Example.com/home, Example.com/welcome, Example.com/index

Homepage Redirecting

If we find a duplicate URL of the homepage and have determined which version to go for, provided that we have the necessary access, we will be implementing the 301 homepage redirect to our recommended version.

Website Logo Alt Text Optimization

Website Logo Alt Text Composition Analysis

Used with the img src http tag, Alt Text provides search engines an important way of understanding what the image is about.

We will be checking whether or not the site's existing website logo's alt text is utilized and properly optimized. We only do this on the banner/logo since this is generally an image that can be seen on ALL pages within the site -- This makes the area very visible to search engines.

We can add optimized alt texts to the rest of the images within the pages of your choosing for an additional charge per alt text.

Website Logo Alt Text Optimization

If the site's existing website logo's alt text is not utilized and properly optimized, we will be creating/recommending an alternate text (alt text) for the website's logo.

Given that the image/logo is located at the topmost part of the source code, there is a very high chance that this will be picked up by search engines. Placing optimized text within the alt text attribute will help the pages rank.

To compose the necessary alt text, the keywords that represent the site as a whole and the primary targeted keywords are taken into consideration along with the company/website's name and the geographic targets.

Robots.TXT Checking & Fixing

Part of our On Page optimization procedure is to check the website for issues concerning its robots.txt file and/or our target pages' robot meta tags.

The robots.txt file provides instructions about the site to web robots such as search engine crawlers (http://www.robotstxt.org/ robotstxt.html). The special HTML <META NAME="ROBOTS" CONTENT=""> tag can also be used to tell robots not to index the content of a page, and/or not scan it for links to follow (http://www.robotstxt.org/meta.html).

Page Title Optimization

The page title appears on the browser's title bar and serves as the link that users click on when they are viewing the search engine results page (SERP). Search engines read the title tag and relate it to the page's content.

The title tag will be optimized in a way that it contains the target keywords and is eye catching at the same time.

Meta Description Optimization

The meta description is typically composed of one or two sentences that describe the page content. A good meta description should be relevant and unique to the page and should reinforce the page title.

Optimizing this meta tag is important because it may appear on the search engine results page (SERP) below the page title. It will be written in a way that it is appealing to users and keyword relevant for search engines.

Uploading of Optimized Meta Tags

Once the Page Title & Meta Descriptions have been created, if we have the necessary access, we will upload the optimized Meta Tags to their corresponding target pages.

Content Analysis and Optimization Guidelines

When we analyze your website during the URL mapping process, we will determine the target page for each keyword. Once we establish the target page for each keyword, we will analyze the content on that page to see if the content has enough words (400 words minimum), and also to see if the content is relevant to the keyword.

Many times you do not have a page established for a particular keyword, and in this instance we would recommend a new page creation.

Most websites require a significant amount of additional content and this content can be written for you or provided by you. We will supply you with a report to show you what pages need content, and what the content needs to be written about (keyword-wise anyways).

Keyword Optimization of Existing Website Content

If a target page has at least 400 words of unique content, it will be keyword-optimized. We make sure that we integrate the target keywords seamlessly and naturally into the existing content.

Unless specified and paid for, this process does not involve fixing any writing issues found in the original content.

Content Uploading

Uploading/Updating the target page with optimized content:

When website content is supplied (either by us or you) and is determined to have passed our keyword requirements, the content will then be uploaded to the live target page.

Promo Call to Action Installation

If applicable, we will be writing promotional content on a monthly basis. As part of most marketing campaigns we ask you to come up with promotions you are willing to offer to your customers/clients. These promotions will be published in many different channels, but specifically published on your blog in the category "Promotions".

In order for users on your website to find your latest promotions we need to install a "Promotion Call to Action" on your website.

Typically this is in the form of a banner we create and upload to the sidebar or footer area of your website. This way, when site users are on your primary website pages they can still reference an image link to find your latest promotions.

Promotions are extremely important to online marketing campaigns and have always been a staple to every large brick and mortar business in the world.

XML Sitemap Analysis, Generation & Installation - Google & Bing

XML Sitemap Generation

An XML Sitemap is a special file that provides search engines with specific directives about what pages to crawl and how often.

If the site does not have an existing, auto-updated XML Sitemap, we will be creating one using various XML sitemap generator tools. If the site's CMS permits, we will be installing a sitemap generator plug-in/ module to make sure that it's auto-updated.

XML Sitemap Installation

Once the XML Sitemap has been created successfully, it will be uploaded to the website's root directory. Sitemap Generation and Installation is done each time our optimizations involve a change to the URL structure of the website.

XML Sitemap Uploading to Google Webmaster

Google Webmaster is a program that webmasters can use to help Google index their contents using XML Sitemaps. After the XML Sitemap is installed on the site, we will then submit it to Google Webmaster for verification.

XML Sitemap Uploading to Bing Webmaster

Bing Webmaster Tools is Bing's Google Webmaster counterpart. After the XML Sitemap is installed on the site, we will also be submitting it to Bing Webmaster for verification.

Google Analytics Script Analysis, Generation & Installation (Target Pages & Homepage)

Google Analytics Script Analysis

Google Analytics is a web analytics tool offering detailed visitor statistics. The tool can be used to track all the usual site activities: visits, page views, pages per visit, bounce rates, average time on the site, and much more. It is an in-depth traffic analytics program.

We will be checking the site for an existing and working Google Analytics (GA) script. What we find will determine whether or not we need to generate a GA code for the site.

Google Analytics Script Generation*

Generating a Google Analytics (GA) script for the site:

If the site does not have a GA script or the client prefers we replace the existing one, then we will generate the GA script for the website. The code generated will later be installed on the site.

Google Analytics Script Installation*

Installing the Google Analytics (GA) script to the site:

The generated GA script will be added to the site's source code. This will be used to track user interactions with the website via the Google Analytics dashboard.

Google Webmaster Script Generation & Installation

Google Webmaster Script Analysis

After 2 to 3 weeks, or once Google Webmaster has enough data, we will then go in and analyze Google Webmaster to make sure your website is indexing properly, malware free, and crawl error free.

Google Webmaster Script Generation*

Google Webmaster allows you to obtain data about crawling, indexing and search traffic. It also allows you to receive notifications about problems on your site. Consequently, we will be generating a new Google Webmaster verification file for the site to gather valuable information that enables us to:

1. Find out how Google crawls, indexes and ranks your site.
2. See how many people found your site in the search results, and how many people clicked on it.
3. Detect if your site has malware or generates errors.
4. See other sites that are linking to yours.
5. Tell Google about your site - submit Sitemaps and see how many pages we added to the index.

Google Webmaster Script Installation*

Installation of the Google Webmaster Script is done either through uploading an HTML file to the site's root directory or adding a meta code on the site's homepage. This will depend on what's applicable to the website access granted.

Google Webmaster Geographic Target Setting, Preferred Domain
Setting the geographic target of a website on Google Webmaster:

This is done via Google Webmaster Tools upon completing the verification process. The country targeted by the website will be assessed through the website's content and the campaign documents. This will help increase the relevance of the website in a particular location.

Website Malware and Virus Check
Diagnosing the site for malware, viruses or other malicious entities:

The site's behavior will be manually analyzed and its files will be thoroughly diagnosed using malware and virus scanners. This is to ensure that the site is functional and is being indexed normally by search engines.

Should they prefer that we fix the issue for them, additional fees apply and we will also be needing the website's back-end access.

Pre & Post Optimization Website Backup

Pre-Optimization Website Backup

Creating a local backup of the website before any On Page optimization:

All downloadable website files will be saved and secured locally before we implement any On Page optimizations.

Post-Optimization Website Backup

Creating a local backup of the website after any On Page optimization:

All downloadable website files will be secured locally after a session of on page optimization is completed. This will serve as a saving point and will aid in tracking and troubleshooting if any issues are encountered in the future.

1 Year Secure Backup Storage*

This will ensure that the backup copy of the website will be secured and will not be removed from our server for an entire year.

Dedicated IP Services

We will provide a dedicated IP for link building purposes. We do this to ensure the link building quality and increase the likelihood of approval for the links we are building. This is because having a dedicated IP allows for a higher approval percentage of the links we build and increases the indexing power behind those links in the major search engines.

IP services will also be utilized when creating your accounts.

Internal Report Auditing and Analysis

All Reporting is subjected to a monthly routine auditing and assessment process. We perform this auditing on a monthly basis to assure that all reports are up to date, error-free, and properly formatted.

The auditing process includes, but is not limited to, the checking of the following:

1. Format
2. Link status analysis
3. 100% of the month's work is completed in full
4. Report is updated accordingly
5. Fixing of errors or dead links

Work Reports

All tasks will be tracked throughout the whole month and are reflected on the monthly report, which includes all progress and final outcomes.

Google Webmaster Error Checking & Reporting

Google Webmaster Error Checking

This serves as a quarterly health check-up on the site that includes web design, site and Meta tags errors, which were not covered in the target pages of the site, and are gathered from Google Webmaster and other tools.

Google Webmaster Error Report

If we find a crawl error on the site, we will be forwarding it to you along with any solutions we have for fixing it.

The reported URLs typically need to be redirected to either the homepage or their new counterpart URLs. Alternatively, they can be blocked using the robots.txt file and reported to Google for removal. The first redirect option is preferred and has more benefits in terms of SEO.

Unique Content Writing (350-400 words - see content type options below)

Google has always said, "Content is King." We write content on an ongoing monthly basis to expand your website, keep the content updates to the website fresh, and create an ongoing "social buzz" about your website. When we create new content, we strategically link it up to other pages in our internally documented content siloing outline. The content is posted to the blog, monthly. The type of content we write depends on the type of content you want us to write. We have a content type scheduler that allows you to go in and choose what type of content you want us to write, as well as what keywords you want us to write about in those content types. You may also input specific notes you want us to focus on or highlight in those content types.

The four primary types of content we write are:
- Company Updates
- Press Releases
- Promotions
- General Information

Press Release

Ongoing monthly content involves writing a fully optimized Press Release that represents your company's special events and promotions or important business updates.

Press Releases are a great way of exposing your brand through interesting or important news and happenings in and around your business that you'd like to share with your target market and audience. Through Press Releases, you are able to announce any company changes using mainstream media outlets. Press Releases rank incredibly well in the search engines and provide you with a great media outlet tool for your company events, promotions and other business updates that you'd like to share with the general public.

The syndication of these Press Releases provides essential, strong back links to our target pages via keyword anchor text. Our Press Releases are individually strategized and linked back to the corresponding pages of the website.

Company Updates

Company updates are pretty much what you would expect them to be. When we write fresh content for your blog on a monthly basis, we want to write about something regarding your company that is both appealing to your social and website audience. Company updates provide us content for amazing blog articles that your target audience will really enjoy reading. In your content scheduler and intake portal, you will be able to tell us what is going on with your company so we know when we can put this information into a company update blog article.

Promotion

Promotions are important for any company, especially with regard to online marketing. Most people looking around the Internet are not especially interested in anything other than what they are specifically searching for. However, if someone is online and might be curious about your services or products, then a promotion would surely attract their attention.

Promotions are time sensitive and prompt people to take action by making a purchase, redeeming a reward, or transacting with the business in the prescribed mechanics to take advantage of the discount, savings or other perks offered within the limited duration. With your input, we will write about your promotions and publish them for you.

General Information

This blog post will focus on general news and information that is directly relevant to the company's product, service, or industry. It is not primarily intended to sell a product or service or to talk about the company. It is a piece that discusses the source material and how it's related to the company's products and services and written in second or third person POV. Possible sources include news and media organizations, industry authorities, and thought leaders.

Uploading Content to Blog

The "unique content" written will be in the form of either a press release, company update, promotion, or industry news. This content will then be uploaded to the appropriate blog category in the blog on your website. We will make sure the blog content is properly displaying and formatted at the basic level.

Categorizing and Tagging Content in Blog

When we upload the written content to your blog we will make sure to properly categorize and tag it. Tags are descriptive comma separated words that describe the written content. These tags will be keyword optimized tags to help with the SEO strategy.

Interlinking Blog Page to Target and Related Pages

When we upload the blog article, we will make sure to interlink the blog article to the respective target page. Blog articles are written with the intent of supporting the primary target pages we have created. Therefore the keywords used in the blog articles will reflect the same keyword subject matter of the keywords on the primary target page it will be interlinked to. By interlinking keyword related blog articles on a monthly basis we are expanding each content silo on the website monthly, and over time, the website could become an authority in the search engines based on content alone.

Blog Article Page Title and Meta Tag Writing & Uploading

When writing blog articles, it is important to keep in mind that you also need to create a descriptive and keyword relevant page title and meta description. Each blog article we write for you will also have a page title and meta description written.

Promotion or News Image Placement (*if applicable)

If you selected to have us write about a promotion or General Information in a particular month, we will be placing an image in the content we write. If you selected to have us write about a promotion for your company then we would generate a graphically designed "coupon" with a bar code and place it within the blog post about the promotion.

If you selected to have us write about General Information then we would "clip" General Information and show an image of the General Information we are writing about on the blog article.

Social Media Distribution

We write fresh content for you on a monthly basis and we need a way to tell the world about this content. The content is uploaded to your blog and we would claim authorship over the written content with your related Google+ account. We let the world know about your newly created content through the 10 social media accounts we have set up for you. We will go into each account and make a "post" or "update" letting everyone know about the newly created content. Of course, we will not say "Hey look at my new content".. we would be letting people know that either a new company update, press release, promotion, or General Information article has been posted and to check it out.

Social media content distribution generates additional social buzz and sends traffic to your blog. We can also generate back links doing this. Ideally this would also generate social signals to your blog articles in the form of Facebook likes, Google+1's etc, however this is dependent on the users actions.

Social Sharing Distribution

Once we have written fresh content for your blog, we want to share it with the outside world. What better way to share newly created content than through social sharing. Social sharing websites are established for the purpose of telling everyone about the content you prefer online and then others can also see it. The nice thing about social sharing is the ability to have others go to what you've shared and add it to their "sharing list" and then everyone who sees their sharing list would also see your page and it could go viral. Social sharing is a no brainer for telling the world about new content online and also builds back links. We will use the social sharing accounts we set up during month 1 for this process.

Off-Site Blog Distribution

When you have multiple blogs you'll want to keep your audience updated on all your fresh content. We will be setting up 6 blogs for you. One of those blogs is on your website, and 5 of the blogs are on outside third party websites as stated in the month 1 line items. When we post new content on your blog we make sure to go into your other 5 external blogs and make a post to let people know about the new content on your blog. They will be able to read part of the content but would need to continue to your website to finish reading the piece of content. By posting notices about new content to your external blogs we are able to keep your external blogs fresh, up to date, and build back links to your website.

Press Release Publications (*if applicable)

Press Releases are submitted to press release publication websites across the global Internet. The publication of the press releases is all done manually. When submitting press releases (depending on the publication site) the keywords targeted in the press release have anchor text pointing back to the target page on your website. The press release is properly categorized, tagged, and submitted to meet the publication date deadline.

The purpose of submitting press releases is to build high quality back links to the target URL of your website, establish a greater branding presence online, and inform the public of a point of significance within your company.

Dedicated IP Services

We will provide a dedicated IP for link building purposes. We do this to ensure the link building quality and increase the likelihood of approval for the links we are building. This is because having a dedicated IP allows for a higher approval percentage of the links we build and increases the indexing power behind those links in the major search engines.

IP services will also be utilized when creating your accounts.

Internal Report Auditing and Analysis

All Reporting is subjected to a monthly routine auditing and assessment process. We perform this auditing on a monthly basis to assure that all reports are up to date, error-free, and properly formatted.

The auditing process includes, but is not limited to, the checking of the following:

1. Format
2. Link status analysis
3. 100% of the month's work is completed in full
4. Report is updated accordingly
5. Fixing of errors or dead links

Website Audit Reports

Here are our Website Audit Reports Packages designed to help your business succeed further.

Manual and Software Driven Keyword Research

Manual Keyword Mining

Before launching a marketing campaign we need to know what keywords to target. A "keyword" is what we refer to as the word or phrased typed into a search engine to return search results. Utilizing software and several man hours of filtering through the Google data, we return a full keyword report. The report not only shows keyword traffic, but also competition analysis and where the website is currently ranking in Google, Yahoo, and Bing for that particular keyword. The keywords chosen determine the direction of the entire marketing campaign, thus the extreme importance we place on keyword research.

Keyword Ranking Report

Keyword Rankings, or where your site is ranked in search engines for keywords, has a major impact on your Web traffic, lead generation and conversions. Research shows more than 75% of all search engine users click on a result on the first page; so the higher you rank in the search engine results pages, the better your chances are of gaining more traffic.

Using specialized software, the rankings of the target keywords for the website will be generated and tabulated. The results will be used as a reference point for the initial rankings of the keywords before the marketing campaign is commenced.

Keyword Structuring

The keywords chosen for the SEO campaign will be analyzed and grouped together. When we group together keywords we will be classifying them as primary or secondary keywords. The keywords will be grouped together based on relevancy. The most competitive keyword of the keyword group will be the primary keyword and all others will be secondary keywords.

Ranking Analysis

We will check every keyword to know the baseline ranking status and so as to determine the ranking URLs. To further determine the competition level of a keyword, we have to manually check your keyword rankings to make sure we know 100% where your website is currently ranking. It is also important to manually check rankings to help us determine target URLs per keyword.

Competition Analysis

We analyze the competition on a given keyword you want to target. It is important for us to look at the competition to have a better understanding of the keyword competition level.

Platform

There are a lot of website platforms. The website can be of pure HTML, ASP, and PHP or is built using a Content Management System like WordPress. However, not all will appear to be search engine or user-friendly. It is important to know this first so that there's nothing that can hinder or limit all required adjustments in the optimization process.

In rare instances, the website may be built on a platform that does not allow us to perform SEO and in that situation; we would be recommending to redesign the website before moving forward with SEO.

On-Site Blog Setup and Configuration

Since search engines love fresh and unique content, we will check if you have an existing blog and if it is properly configured. A blog is primarily important in SEO because it helps you build relationships with your readers, position yourself as an expert in the field, and provide new content for search engines to index.

Malware Check

If a website is infected with malware, then it could hinder its search engine rankings. It is important to make sure the website does not have any malware installed on it, because malware can infect visitors to your website as well.

Website Design General Recommendations

When we analyze the website, we will look at the design components as well. This is not an in-depth analysis, but a light overview. Typically, it is clear if a website requires a "face-lift" in order to reduce bounce rates. The website should be attractive, and clearly display the purpose of the website and the nature of the products or service. The website should also be easy to navigate.

Site Performance

The site performance will be checked in terms of page loading time. The page loading time is one of the important ranking factors that's why checking this is necessary. If a page loads too slowly, then your visitors may leave your website. Google has also placed more importance on page load speed as part of their ranking algorithm. According to Google, if your website loads too slowly, it will negatively impact your rankings. When we find a website that has a slow page load speed we will take the necessary steps to investigate. Often times, it has something to do with the hosting provider.

Navigation Crawlability (Alt Text)

Main navigation is checked to know if it is crawlable or not. Preferably, the navigation should be built in pure HTML text and not on images or JavaScript. This is mainly because Google is not able to read images or JavaScript as navigation elements as of yet. And since the context of the main navigation serves as the primary title of the whole category or theme, then it is important that search engines are able to read the text within the navigation. If the navigation is built using images, then we will also suggest the addition of image alt texts.

Content Crawlability

Content or the main article content is the most important part of a page and it is important to be crawlable by search engines. What can hinder bots from crawling the content is when the site is made up of flash or the content is hidden by JavaScript.

Hosting Check

Upon launching of the site, the hosting should be checked to ensure that the website is safe from any potential malware attacks. We can also determine if a group of sites are hosted on the same server and have the same IP address which is not preferable in terms of SEO, especially when dealing with the same niches.

Search Engine Metrics

We will check to see if there are any existing Webmaster Tools and Analytics installed on the website. If there are no analytics tracking services or webmaster services installed on the website, then we will go ahead and install Google Analytics and Google Webmaster tools. As part of our analysis of the website, we need to be able to check Google Webmaster, as well as Google Analytics.

Sitemaps

There are two types of sitemaps: One is the user sitemap that can be found on the website that helps in guiding users, while the other is the XML sitemap. We are primarily concerned with the XML sitemap. An XML sitemap is generated for use by search engines, to make sure that they can send their crawler bots to all of your pages. If a search engine cannot find all of your pages, then there is no way for those unfound pages to be indexed. XML sitemaps are extremely important and we will make sure yours are installed properly or we will take notes to make sure this is accomplished during on-page optimization.

URL Structure
By organizing the URLs, it will also helps organize the entire website. By having a proper URL structure, it will help users to easily determine what page they are on by just looking at the URL alone.

Most websites do not have a proper url structure and simple put all pages as a direct extension off the homepage.

Lets look at an example of a pesticide company that has 5 different services.

Wrong URL structure:
hompage.com
hompage.com/service1
homepage.com/service2
homepage.com/service3
homepage.com/service4
homepage.com/service5

Correct URL structure:
homepage.com
hompage.com/service/1
homepage.com/service/2
homepage.com/service/3
homepage.com/service/4
homepage.com/service/5

The search engines can only interpret a website as well as it is built. Having properly structured URLs is essential to ensure maximum rank-ability of your website.

Broken Links

Broken links are links that lead to pages that do not exist. When clicking on a broken link, the page you land on is called a 404 error page, it is a standard HTTP response that indicates that the requested URL doesn't exist.

What do you do when you happily surf the web and suddenly come across a 404 error? For most of us, the immediate response would be to simply leave the current site in favor of another one. People and search engines consider broken links as unprofessional.

404 errors and broken links also have negative effects on your search engine rankings so it is quite reasonable to be proactive in avoiding them to improve exposure and increase site traffic. We will look for all the broken links on your website and will report back to you what will be required to fix all of them.

Crawl Errors

These are normally URLs that search engines could not successfully crawl or access. We generally check for 404 (Not Found) errors, which are returned when search engines try to visit a page that does not exist. The common reason for Crawl Errors is that because the page has been deleted, renamed without implementing proper redirection to the new page, or a typographical error. On the other hand, if we see that there are 403 and 500 URL errors, we also include them in the report. But since these are resolved by fixes to the Web server software, we usually just request these errors to be removed from Google.

Custom 404 Error Pages

A custom 404 Error Page informs the visitors that the page cannot be found. It also helps keep them on the site and helps them find the information they're looking for.

Robots.TXT

This is a .txt file that is uploaded on the website and on the Webmaster tools that gives instructions to bots on what to crawl and not to crawl or what pages to index and what not to include in the index. This is helpful in blocking irrelevant pages or directories that is not part of the main informative pages of the site. We will check if this is already existing on the site or not, and we will give proper recommendations according to our findings. A misplaced robots.txt could de-index the entire website in the search engines; so of course, this is a very important step in our auditing process.

Robots Meta Tags

This is another form of Robots.txt. The only difference is how they are uploaded on the website. This one is part of the meta tags that gives instructions to the crawlers on what pages to follow or a no-follow or to index or a no-index. This works the same as Robots.txt but instead of being a site-wide instruction, it is a page-specific instruction. We will check if this already exists on the site and will make sure that it is configured properly.

Number of Indexed Pages vs. Actual Page Count

We will check how many of your web pages are already indexed in Google versus the total amount of pages. This can also help in determining what version (www or non-www) of your URL is good to optimize. If your website has 500 actual pages, but Google says they have only indexed 100 pages of your website, then we need to start our detective work. It is important for Google to index 80%+ of your pages, and if they are indexing less than 80% of your pages, then we need to find out the reasons why they are not indexing more of your pages.

Other Issues

In our audit, we also find issues that do not fall on any of the line items. In such cases, we also include them in our report because sometimes when we fix those issues, other issues that are part of our audit line items also get fixed.

Page Title and Meta Tag Troubleshooting Report

These are basically the parts of a meta tag group. Each page should have a unique set of meta tags since each should represent the contents of the page. We will be checking the duplicates and short meta descriptions and providing proper recommendations for improvement. Having a good meta tag will help increase the click through rate of the pages on the SERP and increase the likelihood of pages to rank higher on the search engines.

Backlink Analysis
This is basically counting the existing backlinks on the website so that we know the baseline and allows us to determine how many backlinks have been built during the active SEO campaign. This will be documented to show the difference and improvement.

Note: For websites with existing backlinks, there is a possibility that those backlinks will get deindexed or devalued by Google and we do not have control over that since we are not the ones whom have been building those existing backlinks. In these instances, please be reminded that it would cause ranking fluctuations.

Duplicate Website Content Checking (Non-Target Pages)
We will check your website for duplicate content and provide a duplicate content report if any exists. If you hired someone to write your website, are you 100% sure it is unique content? Many

copywriters simply rewrite or blatantly copy content from other websites. It is of extreme importance to have original, unique content on your website. If we detect significant duplicate content, we usually require the content to be rewritten in order to ensure maximum rank-ability of your website.

Additional Website Content Writing Requirements

When we analyze your website during the URL mapping process we will determine the target page for each keyword. Once we establish the target page for each keyword, we will analyze the content on that page to see if the content has enough words (400 words minimum) and also to see if the content is relevant to the keyword. Many times, you do not have a page established for a particular keyword, and in this instance we would recommend a new page creation. Most websites require a significant amount of additional content and this content can be written for you or provided by you. We will supply you with a report to show you what pages need content, and what the content needs to be written about (keyword-wise anyways).

Keyword Grouping

This is where we group the target keywords that have been agreed upon into sets of 1-3 keywords, which will then be designated to target pages during the URL Mapping stage. Keywords of a given campaign are grouped based on, but not limited to, similar keywords, related terms, and geo-target.

URL Mapping

If an SEO campaign has 30 keywords, they will not all go on the same page. We usually target 1 keyword on each page, with unique exceptions to the homepage. The process of determining which page should contain certain keywords is URL mapping.

Factors such as theme relevance and page rankings will come into play when URL mapping is performed. Among the target pages that are prioritized are those that are convertible and/or will catch a user's attention, engaging them and encouraging them to interact and browse through the site. The homepage, which is the most highly evaluated page among all the others, is always targeted. If a page with a matching theme does not exist for certain keywords, then a new page with fresh content will have to be created.

Target URLs

The Target URLs are determined during keyword URL mapping. These URLs are simply the pages we are primarily targeting with our On Page and Off Page optimization efforts. When we track the keyword rankings, these are the pages you should see rankings respective to the keywords targeted on each page.

URL Architecture Instructions

This is a set of instructions or recommendations generated from the URL Structure analysis results. This contains a step-by-step process on what needs to be done to properly architect your URLs and what are the concerned pages that need to be fixed. This also contains the instructions on how to optimize the final target pages that were identified from the analysis part of the process.

Website Audit Report Summary and Customized Guidelines

When we finish running all of our checks on your website, we will produce an easy to interpret summary report and provide this along with the rest of the audit in a zip file. The error reports, duplicate meta report, and duplicate website content will be in a separate document inside the zip file.

We will do our best to make the summary informative and to the point. We understand that you do not want to sort through all the data we send over, so we will let you know all the important aspects to look for in our summary report. Within the summary, we will also be providing further recommendations. Further recommendations could be anything from telling you that you need a blog, to telling you that you need to re-design your website before starting a marketing campaign.

Keyword Consultation

After performing the website audit, if we have further concerns about the keywords you want to target, we will contact you and go over our concerns in a consulting session.

Social Media Optimization Services

Did you know that social media is a growing source of leads and customers? The amount of time your target market spends on social media is ever-increasing.

Social media is a fast growing space in online marketing as more and more people connect with each other, communicate and share thoughts and feelings about businesses, brands, products and services through status messages, likes, tweets, links, photos, and videos.

Social Media Optimization - Google Social Dominator

Here are our Social Media Optimization - Google Social Dominator Packages designed to help your business succeed further.

Google+ Setup

Google+ Profile Creation & Optimization

Google+ makes connecting on the web more like socializing in the real world. In this platform, you can share your thoughts, links, and photos with the right circles.

Geo-location and credibility is very important for Google. As such, we'll be asking you to provide us with a verified Google Account that we can use to create and/or customize a Personal Google+ Profile. If you do not have one, we can create one on your behalf, preferably a master email account that can be used for other services you obtained for your campaign. In addition, the Google Account you will be providing needs to have pertinent details like your Full Name, Location, and the actual Profile Picture of the account owner. All of these help make the profile more credible.

Once we have the login details for the Google Account, we will create and optimize your profile by inserting target keywords in your 'About' tab.

Banner Customization of Google+ Business Page

Similar to websites, your Google+ Business Page needs personality. We will be customizing your Google+ Business Page's header (the main images that visitors see on top of your profile page) to help you increase the number of friends in your Circles.

We'll be asking you to provide us with the images that we will customize and insert in your Business Page's header.

Banner Image Sourcing, Editing, Resizing, and Customizing

If there is no specific picture that you would like us to use, you could simply give us some directions on the kind of image you'd like the Page to convey. Based on those, we will be collecting different images and incorporating them into the Banner picture.

We will edit and customize these images to fit the Banner concept and apply them. Once we finish with this, the completed Banner picture will be incorporated into a mockup of the Google+ Page, which will be sent back for feedback. After approval, the mockup can be implemented for the live Google+ Page.

Google+ Business Page Creation & Optimization

Google+ expanded its features and it now accepts 'Brand' or 'Company' based accounts or profiles. This means that business and site owners can now promote and brand their companies within Google+. This may seem like a small change, but one only has to look at the tremendous success of Facebook's fan pages to see why this move is very important for companies and site owners.

While Google+ doesn't come anywhere near the numbers Facebook has, it does hold one major trump card in its hand, the Google brand itself. On the web, immediately building trust with your potential customers is vital for your overall success. Building a large community via Google+ will definitely help in this regard.

We will be creating and/or optimizing a Google+ Business Page for your brand or company to increase your website or company's online visibility.

Branded Content Writing for Google+ Profile Page

First impressions are crucial, and for many, Google+ may be the first instance where they encounter your brand. To give them a proper introduction, the content of the page must be consistent with how the brand is displayed elsewhere.

We will be writing branded content to post on your Google+ Page based on any information about your company we can get from your website or the launch information you provide, with particular attention to the 'About Us' section, to give customers a proper introduction to the company or business.

Google + Profile Information Population

Credibility is important in the world of social networking, and that credibility can be measured partly by how easily people can get to know you. Sharing information about yourself is a great place to start. For the Google+ Profile, we will be uploading information and contact details that are sent to us for specific use there.

YouTube Channel Creation & Optimization

YouTube is undoubtedly the most popular video site today. Millions of people use this service, and it is a great way to provide your videos with a platform to get noticed.

We will create an account for you on YouTube, if one is not already provided, and optimize it by filling out the proper information and making sure it is as informative as possible.

YouTube Channel Design w/ Image Sourcing, Editing, Resizing, and Customizing

To make your YouTube Channel much more appealing and give it branding, we will create a background design for it to convey the company's brand. If we do not get high-resolution images from you, we can base it off the company's website or any specific instruction provided to us. With that, we will source images, edit them as needed, and create a background design for the channel to give it that extra 'wow' factor. Should you have any particular theme or topic in mind for videos, we'll need one month notification ahead of time with complete information to ensure the request can be accommodated.

Branded Content Writing for YouTube Channel

Although videos convey your company's message on YouTube, some people may not spend the time and bandwidth to view each of your videos. To get an overview of what the videos and the company are all about, they would view the Channel page instead.

This is where Branded Content Writing would be useful. From the name itself, it allows us to brand the company through words and provide people with a quick and easy way to find out what the channel is all about.

YouTube Channel Profile Information Population

Credibility is important in the world of social networking, and that credibility can be measured partly by how easily people can get to know you. Sharing information about you is a great place to start.

For the YouTube Profile, we will be uploading information and contact details that are sent to us for specific use there.

Blogger Setup

Blogger Account Creation and Optimization

One of the most popular blogging platforms, Blogger, formerly known as BlogSpot, has a large community which immediately exposes your blog hence your brand, products, and services to a lot of people. This platform is owned by Google and as such, gets good domain rankings and provides a good SEO push for your website.

We will create an account for you on Blogger, if one is not already provided, and optimize it by filling out the proper information and making sure it is as informative as possible.

Blogger Theme Implementation (Design)

Blogger offers a lot of customization options without having to create new designs from scratch. They offer various themes and color schemes to fit your brand.

We will do this customization to give your Blogger blog the best possible look and feel to convey your brand.

Blogger Profile Information Population

Credibility is important in the world of social networking, and that credibility can be measured partly by how easily people can get to know you. Sharing information about yourself is a great place to start.

For the Blogger Profile, we will be uploading information and contact details that are sent to us for specific use there.

Picasa Setup
Picasa Account Creation and Optimization

Picasa is a web album service owned and operated by Google. This allows you to have a centralized location for all images used in your Google products. For example, all photos uploaded through Google Plus and all photos used in Blogger would end up here.

We will create an account for you on Picasa, if one is not already provided.

Website Social Integration

Social Sharing and Social Interaction Buttons Installed on Website

To increase customer Involvement, it is ideal to give your audience the opportunity to interact with you. Customers who enjoy your company's services and offerings will want to know how to get in touch. While email and customer hotlines are still around, social media is fast becoming a preferred alternative.

To this end, we will also be installing buttons onto your website that will refer customers to your various social media channels.

Installation of Social Sharing and Social Interaction buttons will require that we have access to your site's back end.

Miscellaneous Service Items

Dedicated IP Services

We use dedicated IP Services for your campaign to make sure we do not encounter any problems with the social media site's local security.

Reporting and Auditing

Internal Report Auditing and Analysis

For your convenience, we will make sure that reports will include only relevant information, and that the most significant trends and inferences can be determined from the data.

Work Reports

All tasks will be tracked throughout the whole month and are reflected on the monthly report which includes all progress and final outcomes.

Expect the report to be fully updated at the end of the month.

Google+ Marketing
Google+ Page Updates

Having a Google+ Business Page presents an attractive and inexpensive way to create buzz and build momentum for any product or company. This is especially true when it comes to SEO and getting your brand out there on the web and literally in front of potential markets. The SEO capabilities of Google+ could make it a very useful marketing tool, especially for those businesses that are just starting out and/or have small marketing budgets. The Google+ Business Page can help build your brand's visibility, both in the SERPs and in the real world.

We will make sure that your Google+ Business Page is regularly updated with relevant information, which includes your latest events, specials, and promos.

Google Page updates are created one month before they need to be posted. Information about promotions, events, and specials must be provided one month in advance.

Backlink Building from Page Updates

The updates on the Page are also a great chance to refer people to your website. By posting links to pages explaining your brand and services, we can entice those who visit your page to look at your brand, products, and services and include your offerings in their consumer decisions.

Adding People to Your Circle (Google+ Personal Profile)

Sharing things with different people is nothing out of the ordinary. But sharing the right stuff with the right people may get tricky. With Google+ Circles, putting your friends in appropriate groups or categories is a breeze.

To help build your Google+ Personal Profile, we will be creating Circles and adding people to your Circles.

Adding People to Your Circle (Google+ Business Page)

Sharing things with different people is nothing out of the ordinary. But sharing the right stuff with the right people may get tricky. Google+ Circles makes it easy to categorize your friends or prospective customers based on gender or age. You can effectively promote the appropriate products for different types of people thanks to Google+ Circles.

To help build your brand's visibility, we will be creating Circles and adding people to your Circles.

Page Photo Updates

Making content visually appealing tends to increase its impact. Text-only updates are less enticing than ones that incorporate pictures, and are less likely to have 'Share' value. With Photo Updates, it's easier to get people to pay attention to what you have to say, and get them to keep coming back to see what other messages you have.

YouTube Marketing

Video Creation

YouTube is made for video, so we're going to populate your channel with videos! With the use of photos, we can create informative videos that hype up the company's products and services.

We will give focus and emphasis on the company and new products or services. Another option would be to highlight news/events associated with the company.

In line with Video Creation, we would need high-resolution photos provided by you. If you have no photos, we can source them elsewhere, but they will be more generic than if they came from the business itself.
Initially, we can source these from the website and other locations but it would be best if these photos could be provided, especially if we are to create videos regarding events.

Video Uploading

Once the videos are created, we will upload these onto YouTube for you in an optimized fashion.

Video Title Writing

As part of uploading and optimizing the video, we will write a catchy title for it which would briefly and clearly define what it is all about. At the same time, we will aim to make use of the target keyword in the title.

Video Description Writing

Another part of optimizing the video is through the creation of a description. This would provide users additional information about the video, the company, and the products/services being showcased in the video.

This allows for another opportunity to get the message across to people and make use of keywords as well for SEO purposes.

Backlink Building within Video Description

It is possible to place URLs into the description, albeit without the use of anchor text, so we will take full advantage of this.

Aside from the SEO benefits of this link, it also allows for direct traffic. People watching the video who are interested in the company's products and services can easily go to their website through this link on the description.

Video Keyword Tagging

There is a 'tag' section in the video options of YouTube. As part of the optimization process, we will use the keywords and phrases that best describe the video, and hence, the company as well.

This will help in getting the video searched within YouTube and in search engine results.

YouTube Video Commenting

YouTube users are always known to be very vocal through comments. To make the profile seem more active and engaging, we will do commenting on other videos.

This does not mean spamming other videos with marketing spiels or the like, but simply comment on others to benefit the profile, making it look more real and active on YouTube. This will send additional social signals and give the profile more credibility in the eyes of Google.

Blogger Marketing

Blog Article Writing

We will write and create blog posts for the Blogger account in relation to the company. We can make use of different topics per month which includes products and services, about the company, news about the company, news about the industry, and any other related topic which would benefit the reader and the campaign.

If the website currently has a blog in it, we can use the same topics and ideas found there for these articles. We can rewrite these articles to make sure we avoid having duplicate content.

The main advantage here is that since Blogger is one of the most popular blog platforms, it has a huge community already. This community can be tapped faster with a Blogger account.

Blog Article Editing

As part of article production, we will edit these articles first before sending them for approval or posting to make sure everything is written properly. We will never publish any article without proper editing first to ensure accuracy and relevancy.

Backlinking from Blog Post

Another advantage of having a Blogger account is the fact that this blog will be on a different domain. With that in mind, we can use this to build some backlinks to the main website of the company.

However, we will be very careful not to overdo this to avoid looking spammy.

Inclusion of Photos per Blog Article

A plain text blog is plain old boring. This is why we will make use of appropriate photos to give it more life and to help convey the message of the post as well.

Photos sourced from the website or photos provided by you are much preferred. In the absence of such, we will be using stock photos, though they may be more generic and not very specific to your business. For this reason, images provided by you are always preferred.

Picasa Marketing

Picasa Album Creation

The best way to organize photos in Picasa is to use different albums for different themed photos. We will create such albums as needed. The album titles also provide another opportunity to use the target keywords.

If there is no need to create additional albums for new uploaded photos, we will not create them.

Picasa Upload Photos

We will populate the Picasa profile with photos sourced from the website and with those provided. The main advantage of this is that you will have a centralized location of all photos related to the company which can easily be shared with others.

At the same time, these photos will become available on Google's image search as well.

Photo Description Writing

The last part of optimizing the photo is through the creation of the description. This will give a more in-depth portrayal of the image.

Also, this gives us another opportunity to make use of the target keywords.

Miscellaneous Service Items

Dedicated IP Services

We use dedicated IP Services for your campaign to make sure we do not encounter any problems with the social media site's local security.

Reporting and Auditing

Internal Report Auditing and Analysis

For your convenience, we will make sure that reports will include only relevant information, and that the most significant trends and inferences can be determined from the data.

Work Reports

All tasks will be tracked throughout the whole month and are reflected on the monthly report which includes all progress and final outcomes.

Expect the report to be fully updated at the end of the month.

Google+ Marketing Services Packages

Google+ Page Updates

Having a Google+ Business Page presents an attractive and inexpensive way to create buzz and build momentum for any product or company. This is especially true when it comes to SEO and getting your brand out there on the web and literally in front of potential markets. The SEO capabilities of Google+ could make it a very useful marketing tool, especially for those businesses that are just starting out and/or have small marketing budgets. The Google+ Business Page can help build your brand's visibility, both in the SERPs and in the real world.

We will make sure that your Google+ Business Page is regularly updated with relevant information, which includes your latest events, specials, and promos.

Google Page updates are created one month before they need to be posted. Information about promotions, events, and specials must be provided one month in advance.

Backlink Building from Page Updates

The updates on the Page are also a great chance to refer people to your website. By posting links to pages explaining your brand and services, we can entice those who visit your page to look at your brand, products, and services and include your offerings in their consumer decisions.

Add People to Your Circle (Google+ Personal Profile)

Sharing things with different people is nothing out of the ordinary. But sharing the right stuff with the right people may get tricky. With Google+ Circles, putting your friends in appropriate groups or categories is a breeze.

To help build your Google+ Personal Profile, we will be creating Circles and adding people to your Circles.

Add People to Your Circle (Google+ Business Page)

Sharing things with different people is nothing out of the ordinary. But sharing the right stuff with the right people may get tricky. Google+ Circles makes it easy to categorize your friends or prospective customers based on gender or age. You can effectively promote the appropriate products for different types of people thanks to Google+ Circles.

To help build your brand's visibility, we will be creating Circles and adding people to your Circles.

Page Photo Updates

Making content visually appealing tends to increase its impact. Text-only updates are less enticing than ones that incorporate pictures, and are less likely to have 'Share' value. With Photo Updates, it's easier to get people to pay attention to what you have to say, and get them to keep coming back to see what other messages you have.

Facebook Setup and Design - Profile Creation & Optimization

Facebook, the social network that's 'free and always will be," is widely regarded as the most dominant social network. Here, you can share thoughts, ideas, pictures, and links to sites and articles that are near and dear to your heart.

To start, we'll be asking for accurate details that we can use to start building your corner of the social network. These include an Email Address, the Full Name of the designated account owner, the person's Location, and a Profile Picture. Target keywords can also be inserted into the 'About' section of the profile upon request.

If there is already a Facebook Profile that you would like us to use, we would need to ask for the access details for it (Username and Password), and we will be optimizing it for added visual appeal and target audience impact.

Banner Customization of Facebook Profile
With the new Timeline view, users are given the opportunity to give their own visual flavor to their profile. We will be customizing your Facebook Profile banner (the main image that visitors see on top of your profile page) to help you maximize the number of friends you can get.
We'll be asking you to provide us with the images that we will customize and insert in your Facebook Profile's header.

Banner Image Sourcing, Editing, Resizing, and Customizing

If there is no specific picture that you would like us to use, you could simply give us some directions on the kind of image you'd like the Profile to convey. Based on those, we will be collecting different images and incorporating them into the Banner picture.

We will edit and customize these images to fit the Banner concept and apply them. Once we finish with this, the completed Banner picture will be incorporated into a mockup of the Facebook profile, which will be sent back for feedback. After approval, the mockup can be implemented for the live Facebook Profile.

Facebook Business Page Creation & Optimization

Aside from personal profiles, Facebook allows businesses to have their own Business Pages to interact with customers. Announcements on upcoming events, sales, discounts and other offerings can be made. Many businesses have also found Pages to be useful for getting customer feedback; loyal and satisfied customers can post positive testimonials here.

Setting up a Page on Facebook will evidently be helpful in increasing your online visibility. If the content of the page is appealing enough to the target audience, it can also be very helpful in getting additional customers.

Facebook Business Page Design w/ Image Sourcing, Editing, Resizing, and Customizing

Similar to the Facebook Profile, we will be using images to make the Page more attractive to visitors. If necessary, a color scheme that fits with the brand will be followed. The company or business logo will be incorporated, and niche-oriented pictures will also be used. We will also be asking if there are specific pictures that the client would like to use.

A mockup will be created for the Business Page and sent for feedback to the client. Upon approval, the design will be implemented.

Branded Content Writing for Facebook Business Page

First impressions are crucial, and for many people, Facebook may be the first instance where they encounter your brand. To give them a proper introduction, the content of the page must be consistent with how the brand is displayed elsewhere.

We will be writing branded content to post on your Business Page, with particular attention to the 'About Us' section, to give customers a proper preview of the company or business. It is also important to assure loyal customers that your voice is the same, no matter where they find you.

Facebook Profile Information Population

Credibility is important in the world of social networking, and that credibility can be measured partly by how easily people can get to know you. Sharing information about yourself is a great place to start.

For the Facebook Profile, we will be uploading information and contact details that are sent to us for specific use there.

Branded Content Writing for Facebook Business Page SEO Tab

The Business Page SEO tab provides a quick overview of the company, its background, and its products/services. We will create branded content for the tab to include the targeted keywords in order to promote its products/services.

The information we will use for this will be from the live website of the company. If this is not available, we will need to request for the company's background and product/service information.

Social Sharing and Social Interaction Buttons Installed on Website

To increase customer Involvement, it is ideal to give them the opportunity to interact with you. Customers who enjoy your company's services and offerings will want to know how to get in touch. While email and customer hotlines are still around, Social Media is fast becoming a preferred alternative.

To this end, we will also be installing buttons onto your website and blog that will refer customers to your Facebook Business Page.

Installation of Social Sharing and Social Interaction buttons will require that we have access to your site's back end.

Facebook Marketing Services Packages

Facebook Profile Updates

With regular profile updates, we will ensure that your Facebook profile has credibility and presence on the social network. An online presence cannot be successfully established without activity.

Facebook profile updates will be posted to the Personal Facebook profile, which is the account used to join groups and send friend requests. They will not be posted to the Facebook Page. Updates are to be created one month before they have to be posted.

Backlink Building from Profile Updates

Profile updates are also a good opportunity to generate traffic into your site. By incorporating links to your site into updates, we increase the chances of people visiting your website, where they can learn more about your services and offerings.

Facebook Commenting and Discussion

We start or participate in various discussions. This can be done within a Facebook Group or a Facebook Page that is related to the company's niche.

Backlink Building from Comments

A well-placed backlink in a comment can also successfully channel traffic to your business website. By putting a link in a discussion or thread whose participants may be interested in your niche, there are increased chances for your website to get hits and conversions.

Facebook Groups Joined

Another opportunity to increase your company's reach is to join Facebook Groups. By selecting ones that are targeted to your niche, we can find people that may be interested in availing of your services. Participating in discussions can also be beneficial if you want to be established as an industry authority.

We shall request to join groups that are aimed at your business's niche and/or geographic location.

Facebook Friend Acquisition

For the Profile updates and posts to have an impact, we must acquire Friends. Any updates and posts we publish can appear on a Friend's Newsfeed, which will increase the potential reach of the message.

We shall send requests for people to add the Facebook personal profile as a Friend on Facebook.

Facebook Page Updates

Maintaining activity on the Facebook Business Page is also crucial. With regular updates, Fans of the page can be kept up-to-date on new events, discounts, and offerings your business has. The right content, which is sufficiently interesting or entertaining, can also make them more inclined to visit your Page regularly.

Updates are written one month before they are to be posted. To ensure timely updates about events, discounts, and offerings, we would need information about such announcements one month in advance.

Backlink Building from Page Updates

The updates on the Page are also a great chance to refer people to your website. By posting links to pages explaining your brand and services, we can entice Fans to look them up and include your offerings in their consumer decisions.

Photo Updates

Making content visually appealing tends to increase its impact. Text-only updates are less enticing than ones that incorporate pictures, and are less likely to have 'Share' value. With Photo Updates, people are more likely to pay attention to what you have to say, and they'll keep coming back to see what other messages you have to share.

As with profile and page updates, photo updates are conceptualized one month in advance.

Youtube Setup and Design

YouTube Channel Creation & Optimization

YouTube is undoubtedly the most popular video site today. Millions of people use this service and it is a great way to provide your videos a platform to get noticed.

We will create an account for you on YouTube, if one is not already provided, and optimize it by filling out the proper information and making sure it is as informative as possible.

Unique Email Account Creation (if required)

The creation of a YouTube profile requires a Gmail account. We will create this unique email prior to creating the profile if one is not provided already. At the same time, we will make sure that the Gmail account we create would be branded towards the company/business.

Image Sourcing for Design

We will source images from the website and stock photo sites as needed in order to create the design.

Image Editing and Resizing

We will resize and edit the sourced or provided images in order to fit the design concept for the YouTube channel.

Image Cleaning and Finalizing

We will clean the images as needed in order to get the best look and feel for the design.

Branded Content Writing for Youtube Channel

Although videos convey your company's message on YouTube, some people may not spend the time and bandwidth to view each of your videos. To get an overview of what the videos and the company are all about, they would view the Channel page instead.

This is where Branded Content Writing would be useful. From the name itself, it allows us to brand the company through words and provide people with a quick and easy way to find out what the channel is all about.

We will use information as provided for the content as well as information available on their website.

YouTube Channel Profile Information Population

Credibility is important in the world of social networking, and that credibility can be measured partly by how easily people can get to know you. Sharing information about yourself is a great place to start.

For the YouTube Profile, we will be uploading information and contact details that are sent to us for specific use there.

Social Sharing and Social Interaction Buttons Installed on Website

To increase client Involvement, it is ideal to give them the opportunity to interact with you. Customers who have enjoyed or continue to enjoy your company's services and offerings will want to know how to get in touch. While email and customer hotlines are still around, Social Media is fast becoming a preferred alternative.

To this end, we will also be installing buttons onto your website and blog that will refer customers to your YouTube Page.

Video Creation

YouTube is made for video, so we're going to populate your profile with videos! With the use of photos, we can create informative, commercial type videos that hype up the company's products and services.

We will focus and put emphasis on the company and its new products or services. Another option would be to highlight news/events associated with the company.

In line with Video Creation, we would need high-resolution photos provided by you. If you have no photos, we can source them elsewhere, but they will be more generic than if they came from the business itself.

Photos sourced from the website or photos that are provided by you are much preferred. In the absence of such, we will use stock photos, though they may be more generic and not very specific to your business. For this reason, images provided by you are always preferred.

Video Uploading

Once the videos are created, we will upload these onto YouTube for you in an optimized fashion.

Video Title Writing

As part of uploading and optimizing the video, we will write a catchy title for it which would briefly and clearly define what it is all about. At the same time, we will aim to make use of the target keyword in the title.

Video Description Writing

Another means of optimizing the video is through the creation of a description. This would provide users additional information about the video, the company, and the products/services being showcased in the video.

Video description writing creates another opportunity to get the message across to people, and make use of keywords as well for SEO purposes.

Backlink Building within Video Description

It is possible to place URLs in the description (albeit without the use of anchor texts), and we will take full advantage of this feature.

Aside from the SEO benefits of this link, it also allows for direct traffic. People watching the video who are interested in the company's products and services can easily go to their website through this link on the description.

Video Keyword Tagging

There is a 'tag' section in the video options of YouTube. As part of the optimization process, we will use the keywords and phrases that best describe the video and hence, the company as well.

This will help in getting the video searched within YouTube and in search engine results.

YouTube Video Commenting

YouTube users are always known to be very vocal through comments. To make the profile seem more active and engaging, we will do commenting on other videos.

This does not mean spamming other videos with marketing spiels or the like, but simply comment on others to benefit the profile making it look more real and active on YouTube. This will send additional social signals and give the profile more credibility in the eyes of Google.

Social Sharing and Social Interaction Buttons Installed on Website

To increase client Involvement, it is ideal to give them the opportunity to interact with you. Customers who have enjoyed or continue to enjoy your company's services and offerings will want to know how to get in touch. While email and customer hotlines are still around, Social Media is fast becoming a preferred alternative.

To this end, we will also be installing buttons onto your website and blog that will refer customers to your Youtube Page.

The installation of Social Sharing and Social Interaction buttons will require that we have access to your site's back end.

LinkedIn Setup and Design

LinkedIn Profile Creation & Optimization

LinkedIn, while not as 'fun' as Twitter or Facebook, is an important social network for establishing online presence, especially for professionals. It's regarded as the premiere social networking site for finding business opportunities.

To start, we'll be asking for accurate details that we can use to start building your professional profile. These include an Email Address, the Full Name of the designated account owner, the person's Location, and a Profile Picture. Target keywords can also be inserted into the 'About' section of the profile upon request.

If there is already a LinkedIn profile that you would like us to use, we would need to ask for its access details (Username and Password), and we will be optimizing it for added impact.

Branded Content Writing for LinkedIn Profile

First impressions are crucial, and your LinkedIn profile may be the first opportunity for other professionals to get in touch with your brand. To give them a proper introduction, the content of the page must be consistent with how the brand is displayed elsewhere.

We will be writing branded content to post on your LinkedIn Page, with particular attention to the 'About Us' section, to give prospective contacts a proper preview of the company or business. It is also important to assure longtime contacts that your professional voice is the same, no matter where you are.

LinkedIn Profile Information Population

Credibility is important in the world of social networking, and that credibility can be measured partly by how easily people can learn about you and your business. Sharing information about yourself is a great place to start.

For the LinkedIn Profile, we will be uploading information and contact details that are sent to us for specific use there.

Social Sharing and Social Interaction Buttons Installed on Website

To increase your Involvement, it is ideal to give your audience the opportunity to interact with you. Customers who have enjoyed or continue to enjoy your company's services and offerings will want to know how to get in touch. While email and customer hotlines are still around, social media is fast becoming a preferred alternative.

To this end, we will also be installing buttons onto your website that will refer customers to your LinkedIn Page.

Installation of Social Sharing and Social Interaction buttons will require that we have access to your site's back end.

LinkedIn Marketing Services Packages

LinkedIn Updates

With regular profile updates, we will ensure that your LinkedIn profile has credibility and presence on the social network. An online presence cannot be successfully established without activity. Updates are created one month before they are posted. We must be informed of any preferred themes or subjects for updates at least one month in advance.

Backlink Building from Updates

Updates are also a good opportunity to generate traffic into your site. By incorporating links to your site into updates, we increase the chances of people visiting your website, where they can learn more about your services and offerings.

LinkedIn Discussions

We start or participate in various discussions. This can be done within a LinkedIn Group that is related to the company's niche.

Backlink Building from Discussion

A well-placed backlink in a comment can also successfully channel traffic to your business website. By putting a link in a discussion or thread whose participants may be interested in your niche, there are increased chances for your website to get hits and conversions.

LinkedIn Groups Joined

Another opportunity to increase your company's reach is to join LinkedIn Groups. By selecting ones that are targeted to your niche, we can find people that may be interested in doing business with you. Participating in discussions can also be beneficial if you want to be established as an industry authority.

We shall request to join groups that are related to your business's niche and/or geographic location.

LinkedIn Connections Acquisition

For the updates and posts to have an impact, we must acquire Connections. Any updates and posts we publish can appear on a contact's home page, which will increase the potential reach of the message. Backlinks will also only have an impact if they are read, and the chances of this happening are increased when they become part of someone's LinkedIn home page.

We shall send requests for people to add the LinkedIn profile as a Connection on LinkedIn.

Twitter Setup and Design

Twitter Profile Creation & Optimization

Twitter is a real-time micro-blogging service where mini-messages ('tweets') are sent by users to share their ideas and links to sites they like. The tweets are restricted to 140 characters in length, including spaces, and this has forced many users to find creative ways to get their messages across.

To start, we'll be asking for accurate details that we can use to start building your business' own Twitter page. These include an Email Address, the desired Name of the Twitter profile, the Location of the Business, and a Profile Picture. Target keywords can also be inserted into the 'About' section of the profile upon request.

If there is already a Twitter Profile that you would like us to use, we would need to ask for the access details for it (Username and Password), and we will be optimizing it for added visual appeal and target audience impact.

Background Customization of Twitter Page

By changing the background, Twitter users have the opportunity to put their own visual spin on their profile. We will be customizing your Twitter background (the background image that visitors see when they view your Profile) to help you maximize the number of followers you can get.

We'll be asking you to provide us with the images that we will customize and insert in your Twitter Profile background.

Branded Content Writing for Twitter Page

First impressions are crucial, and for many, Twitter may be the first instance where they encounter your brand. To give them a proper introduction, the content of the page must be consistent with how the brand is displayed elsewhere.

We will be writing branded content to post on your Twitter Page, with particular attention to the 'About Us' section, to give customers a proper preview of the company or business. It is also important to assure loyal customers that your voice is the same, no matter where they find you.

Twitter Page Information Population

Credibility is important in the world of social networking, and that credibility can be measured partly by how easily people can get to know you. Sharing information about yourself is a great place to start.

For the Twitter Profile, we will be uploading information and contact details that are sent to us for specific use there.

Social Sharing and Social Interaction Buttons Installed on Website

To increase customer Involvement, it is ideal to give them the opportunity to interact with you. Customers who enjoy your company's services and offerings will want to know how to get in touch. While email and customer hotlines are still around, Social Media is fast becoming a preferred alternative.

Twitter Marketing Services Packages

Tweets

With regular tweets, we will ensure that your Twitter profile has credibility and presence on the social network. An online presence cannot be successfully established without activity, and this is especially true for Twitter, where real-time updates are the main source of the platform's value.

We'll be creating updates promoting your products or services; tweets are sent one month before they are posted. If there is any specific topic or announcement desired, a notice must be given one month in advance.

Backlink Building from Tweets

Tweets are also a good opportunity to generate traffic to your site. By incorporating links to your site into tweets, we increase the chances of people visiting your website, where they can learn more about your services and offerings.

Twitter Follower Acquisition

For the tweets to have an impact, we must acquire followers. Any tweets we publish will appear on a follower's feed, which will let him or her read your messages. This be especially beneficial for updates with backlinks, where exposure is crucial.

We will follow Twitter profiles that might be interested in your services and may follow your Twitter account back.

Blogger Setup and Design

Blogger Account Creation and Optimization

One of the most popular blogging platforms, Blogger, formerly known as Blogspot, has a large community which immediately exposes your blog, hence your brand, products, and services, to a lot of people. This platform is owned by Google and as such, gets good domain rankings and provide a good SEO push for your website.

We will create an account for you on Blogger, if one is not already provided, and optimize it by filling out the proper information and making sure it is as informative as possible.

Blogger Theme Implementation (Design)

Blogger offers a lot of customization options without having to create new designs from scratch. They offer various themes and color schemes to fit your brand.

We will do this customization to give your Blogger blog the best possible look and feel to convey your brand.

Google+ Authorship Inclusion

One of Google's latest and innovative features is the use of Author tags. Basically, this ties your Google+ profile to the blog post created. Your profile will appear with the post on Google's search results page.

This will give the blog more credibility from Google's point of view, and hence, better ranking results.

Social Sharing and Social Interaction Buttons Installed on Website

To increase your Involvement, it is ideal to give your audience the opportunity to interact with you. Customers who have enjoyed or continue to enjoy your company's services and offerings will want to know how to get in touch. While email and customer hotlines are still around, Social Media is fast becoming a preferred alternative.

To this end, we will also be installing buttons onto your website that will refer customers to your Blogger Page.

Blogger Marketing Services Packages

Blog Article Writing

We will write and create blog posts for the Blogger account in relation to the company. We can make use of different topics per month which includes products and services, about the company, news about the company, news about the industry, and any other related topic which would benefit the reader and the campaign.

If the website currently has a blog in it, we can use the same topics and ideas found there for these articles. We can rewrite these articles to make sure we avoid having duplicate content.

The main advantage here is that since Blogger is one of the most popular blog platforms, it has a huge community already. This community can be tapped faster with a Blogger account.

Blog Article Editing

As part of article production, we will edit these articles first before sending them for approval or posting to make sure everything is written properly. We will never publish any article without proper editing first to ensure accuracy and relevancy.

Backlinking from Blog Post

Another advantage of having a Blogger account is the fact that this blog will be on a different domain. With that in mind, we can use this to build some backlinks to the main website of the company.

However, we will be very careful not to overdo this to avoid looking spammy.

Inclusion of Photos per Blog Article

A plain text blog is plain old boring. This is why we will make use of appropriate photos to give it more life and to help convey the message of the post as well.

Photos sourced from the website or photos provided by you are much preferred. In the absence of such, we will be using stock photos, though they may be more generic and not very specific to your business. For this reason, images provided by you are always preferred.

Picasa Setup and Design
Picasa Account Creation and Optimization

Picasa is a web album service owned and operated by Google. This allows you to have a centralized location for all images used in your Google products. For example, all photos uploaded through Google Plus and all photos used in Blogger would end up here.

We will create an account for you on Picasa, if one is not already provided.

Unique Email Account Creation (if required)

The creation of a Picasa profile requires a Gmail account. We will create this unique email prior to creating the profile if one is not provided already. At the same time, we will make sure that the Gmail account we create would be branded towards the company/business.

Email Verification
As part of the setup process, we will verify the account via email to complete the sign up process. company/business.

Branded Content Writing for Picasa Profile

Your Picasa profile would be under the name of the company. In this sense, it is ideal to have as much information about the company as possible on here so anytime people looks at the pictures or your profile, you get to brand yourself.

We will use information as provided for the content as well as information available on their website.

Note that the Picasa profile information would be based on the G+ account linked to the Picasa profile.

Picasa Profile Information Population

Credibility is important in the world of social networking, and that credibility can be measured partly by how easily people can get to know you. Sharing information about yourself is a great place to start.

For the Picasa Profile, we will be uploading information and contact details that are sent to us for specific use there.

Note that Picasa profile information would be based on the G+ account linked to the Picasa profile.

Dedicated IP Services

We use dedicated IP Services for your campaign to make sure we do not encounter any problems with the social media site's local security.

Internal Report Auditing and Analysis

For your convenience, we will make sure that reports will include only relevant information, and that the most significant trends and inferences can be determined from the data.

Work Reports

All tasks will be tracked throughout the whole month and are reflected on the monthly report, which includes all progress and final outcomes.

Picasa Marketing Services Packages

Picasa Album Creation

The best way to organize photos in Picasa is to use different albums for different themed photos. We will create such albums as needed. The album titles also provide another opportunity to use the target keywords.

If there is no need to create additional albums for new uploaded photos, we will not create them.

Picasa Photo Uploads

We will populate the Picasa profile with photos sourced from the website and with those provided. The main advantage of this is that you will have a centralized location of all photos related to the company which can easily be shared to others.

At the same time, these photos will become available on Google's image search as well.

Photo Photo Description Writing

The last part of optimizing the photo is through the creation of the description. This will give a more in-depth portrayal of the image.

Also, this gives us another opportunity to make use of the target keywords.

Pinterest Setup and Design

Pinterest Account Creation and Optimization

Pinterest is a web photo sharing site that allows you to upload pictures onto your profile. The images can be organized through the use of different boards, and then shared with other Pinterest users.

We will create an account for you on Pinterest, if one is not already provided, and optimize it by filling out the proper information and making sure it is as informative as possible.

Branded Content Writing for Pinterest Profile

Your Pinterest profile would be under the name of the company. Hence, it is ideal to have as much information about your company as possible on your Pinterest profile so that anytime someone looks at the pictures or your profile, you get to present your brand.

We will use information as provided for the content as well as information available on your website.

Social Sharing and Social Interaction Buttons Installed on Website

To increase your Involvement, it is ideal to give your audience the opportunity to interact with you. Customers who have enjoyed or continue to enjoy your company's services and offerings will want to know how to get in touch. While email and customer hotlines are still around, social media is fast becoming a preferred alternative.

Pinterest Marketing Services Packages

Pinterest Board Creation

Boards facilitate the organizing of photos with a similar theme. Boards need to be created before photos can be uploaded, and we will create these to reflect the photo themes.

We will also make sure that the boards are publicly viewable.

Pinterest Photo Pinning (photo uploading)

This is the equivalent of photo uploading onto your Pinterest profile. We will upload these photos and optimize them by giving them proper titles and descriptions. Photos sourced from your website or provided by you are much preferred. In the absence of such, we will be using stock photos, though they may be more generic and not very specific to your business. For this reason, images provided by you are always preferred.

Backlink Building with Photo Pinning

We are able to provide a link, albeit without using anchor text, onto the descriptions of the photos. This is a great way to gather links as well as direct traffic from the uploaded images on Pinterest.

Pinterest Follow Profiles

In order to give the profile more credibility and to keep it active, we will follow other Pinterest profiles as well.

Pay Per Click Advertising

Did you know that PPC is the fastest way to drive instant traffic to your website? What can your website do without traffic? Without traffic, you are losing time, opportunities and money to your competition.

If you are looking for instant traffic and targeting potential customers with online ads that are triggered by search and are set to only appear at a certain time for a specific geographic location, or are set to appear at high traffic websites you selected, then Pay Per Click advertising is for you.

Monthly AdWords Budget Range

Represents the agreed upon, allotted monthly budget for the AdWords campaign.

Website and/or Landing Page Analysis

Relevance of keywords, ad-copies and landing pages is a must for higher visibility in AdWords. Consequently, we will be analyzing the site's landing page/s, target keywords and ad-copies to make sure that each one is relevant to the other.

Competitive Analysis

Analyzing your competitors' AdWords campaigns enables us to know who we are up against and helps us tailor the campaign strategy more effectively. Analysis includes competitor keywords, ads, landing pages & more.

Account Setup

This will involve linking the pre-existing Google Analytics account to the PPC (AdWords) account. Google Analytics tracks and monitors more detailed key metrics to improve performance of an AdWords campaign.

AdWords Tracking Code Setup

Setting up AdWords Conversion Tracking enables you to effectively track and monitor conversions of users who click on the ads. A conversion is simply an action a user takes on your site that has value to your business. Conversion Tracking also enables you to track which of your keywords best leads to clicks and conversions such as sales.

Conversion Tracking works by putting a little snippet of HTML code on the page that users arrive at after they complete a valuable action on your site.

Keyword Research

Our goal at this point is to find the keywords that are most relevant to the campaign's landing pages and PPC ads. As well as relevance, we will be taking factors like monthly search volume and competition into consideration. Keyword research involves the use of Google AdWords' various keyword research tools as well as third party keyword research tools.

Number of keywords per Ad-group

Simply put, every campaign has to have 1 ad group that contains the keywords and the ads that Google will display on the search engine results.

Search Network

AdWords campaigns with keywords are automatically eligible to appear on the Search Network. These ads are targeted based on a user's search terms. For example, if you search for 'Italian coffee' on a search engine powered by Google, such as AOL.com, you'll see related coffee ads next to the search results. Ref: http://adwords.google.com/support/aw/bin/answer.py?hl=en&answer=90956

Display Network

Previously known as the Google Content Network, the Google Display Network includes a collection of websites that have partnered with Google (display partners), YouTube, and specific Google properties that display AdWords ads. Ref: http://adwords.google.com/support/ aw/bin/answer.py?hl=en&answer=117120

Ad groups creation

An Ad group contains one or more ads which target a set of keywords, placements, or both. You set a bid, or price, to be used when your ad is triggered by the keywords or placements in the ad group. This is called a cost per click (CPC) or cost per thousand impressions (CPM) bid. Ref: http://adwords.google.com/support/aw/bin/answer.py? hl=en&answer=6298

We will be creating the best possible ad-groups that are organized thematically to ensure that the campaign can be easily managed and optimized.

Ad-copy creation

A text ad is the primary type of ad in the AdWords program.

Text ads can be shown on Google and across the Google Network, and are sometimes known as 'sponsored links' because the title links to your website.

http://adwords.google.com/support/aw/bin/answer.py? hl=en&answer=14093

A/B Ad copy split-testing

With split testing, two or more ads are tested side by side to determine which performs better at a specific metric, allowing us to make improvements as necessary. Testing campaigns allows you to be aware of what works and what doesn't on your PPC campaign, making it a critical aspect of effective optimization.

http://www.searchmarketingstandard.com/maximizing-ppc-split-testing-strategies

Geo-targeting

Geo-targeting is an AdWords search campaign feature that allows advertisers to restrict ad distribution only to users with an IP address registered at an Internet Service Provider (ISP) with addresses assigned to a Designated Market Area (DMA), manually designated cities, or within a custom radius or polygonal range.

We will be setting the Geo-target of the campaign to ensure that the ads reach only your target market.

Ad scheduling

Ad scheduling lets you specify certain hours or days of the week when you want your AdWords ads to appear. For example, you might schedule your ads to run only on weekdays, or from 3:00 until 6:00 p.m. daily. With ad scheduling, a campaign can be programmed to run every day, or as seldom as 15 minutes per week.

Ad scheduling also includes an advanced setting which lets you adjust pricing for your ads during certain time periods. For example, if you find that your ads get the best results between 8:00 and 11:00 a.m., you can bid more for impressions or clicks during that period.

Ref: http://adwords.google.com/support/aw/bin/answer.py?hl=en&answer=117585

Adwords Campaign Experiments (ACE Test)

AdWords Campaign Experiments (ACE) is a tool that allows you to accurately test and measure changes to your keywords, bids, ad groups, ads, placements and more. ACE allows you to test and measure changes in real-time by executing your experimental campaign alongside your original campaign. By performing this type of simultaneous split test, we can tell you precisely the kind statistical changes your Search and Content campaign changes will produce.

Keyword Matching Options

We will be utilizing the four keyword matching options to help determine which Google searches can trigger your ads to appear. These four matching options can help control who sees your ads:

1. Broad match: keyword Allows your ad to show on similar phrases and relevant variations (The broad match modifier may also be used to further refine your broad keyword matches: +keyword.)

2. Phrase match: 'keyword' Allows your ad to show for searches that match the exact phrase.

3. Exact match: [keyword] Allows your ad to show for searches that match the exact phrase exclusively.

4. Negative match: -keyword Ensures your ad doesn't show for any search that includes that term

With some options, you'll enjoy more ad impressions, clicks, and conversions; with others, you'll get fewer impressions and more narrow targeting. By applying the appropriate matching options to your keywords, you can best meet your ROI goals.

http://adwords.google.com/support/aw/bin/answer.py?hl=en&answer=6100

Budget Management

Your daily budget is the amount that you're willing to spend on a specific AdWords campaign each day. AdWords displays your ads as often as possible while staying within your daily budget. When the budget limit is reached, your ads will typically stop showing for that day. How quickly your ads are shown during a given day is determined by your ad delivery setting.

Ref: http://adwords.google.com/support/aw/bin/answer.py?hl=en&answer=6312

Part of our AdWords campaign management is ensuring that you get the best ads placement possible with the budget you have allotted for your campaign.

Keyword Bid Management

A Keyword Bid is the dollar amount that an advertiser is willing to pay to display an ad relative to the competition. So in essence, Keyword Bid Management is how you control the bids to maximize the aforementioned dollar amount favorable to the advertiser.

Negative Keyword Research

Negative keywords are a core component of a successful keyword list. Adding a negative keyword to your ad group or campaign means that your ads won't show for search queries containing that term.

By filtering out unwanted impressions, negative keywords can help you reach the most appropriate prospects, reduce your cost-per-click (CPC), and increase your ROI.

Ref: http://adwords.google.com/support/aw/bin/answer.py? hl=en&answer=63235

We will be performing keyword research to create a list of the appropriate negative keywords that we'll be using to filter out unwanted impressions.

Enterprise Level PPC Management Platform

Using an enterprise level PPC Management platform helps supercharge paid search campaigns with actionable insights. Monthly analysis and monitoring of the data coming from the Enterprise Level PPC Management Platform enables the PPC Campaign Manager to recommend and implement further improvements to the account's performance.

Conversion Tracking

AdWords Conversion Tracking is a tool to help you measure conversions and ultimately help you identify how effective your AdWords ads and keywords are for you.
Ref: http://adwords.google.com/support/aw/bin/answer.py? hl=en&answer=142348

The monthly analysis and monitoring of this data enables the PPC Campaign Manager to recommend and implement further improvements to the account's performance.

Traffic Statistics Analysis

Adwords traffic analytics, is an Adwords tracking system that reports information on clicks, impressions, CTR (click through rate), conversions, CPC (cost per click) and more.

Effective traffic analysis is key to great campaign performance. The monthly analysis and monitoring of this data enables the PPC Campaign Manager to recommend and implement further improvements to the account's performance.

Search Query Report Analysis

You can see how your ads performed on actual searches within the Search Network on the Campaigns tab. Identify new search terms with high potential that you want to add as keywords and weed out any terms that aren't as relevant to your business.

What's the difference between a search term and a keyword? A search term is the exact word or set of words a user enters when searching on Google.com or one of our Search Network sites. A keyword is the

word or set of words AdWords advertisers create for a given ad group to target their ads to potential customers.
Ref: http://adwords.google.com/support/aw/bin/answer.py? hl=en&answer=68034

Click Fraud Analysis & Support

Click fraud is a type of Internet crime that occurs in pay per click online advertising when a person, automated script or computer program imitates a legitimate user of a web browser clicking on an ad, for the purpose of generating a charge per click without having actual interest in the target of the ad's link.

Proper click fraud analysis & reporting is essential to reducing Adwords costs for the PPC advertisers.

We will help you with detecting click fraud and in reporting anything suspicious immediately to Google. You can learn more about invalid clicks here:

http://adwords.blogspot.com/2006/03/about-invalid-clicks.html

ROI Management

Return on Investment (ROI) is the ratio of the cost of advertising relative to the profit generated from conversions such as sales or leads. Your ROI indicates the value to your business gained in return for the cost of your ad campaign.

The ROI analysis report, which is customized based on your goals for the PPC campaign, is also included in the Enterprise Level Monthly Reports we will be sending you.

Google Analytics Tracking Code Setup

Google Analytics is the enterprise-class web analytics solution that gives you rich insights into your website traffic and marketing effectiveness. Being different from AdWords, Google Analytics enables you to track and monitor customer interaction with your website.

Here, we will be generating the necessary analytics tracking code that can be pasted to any page of your site that you want to track performance on using Google Analytics.

Analysis & Monitoring

PPC data is just a small part of valuable data that Google Analytics provides, albeit very useful in terms of optimizing PPC campaign performance. Effective analysis and monitoring of this data coming from Analytics is another avenue for the PPC campaign manager to be able to recommend and implement further improvement to the account's performance.

Enterprise Level Weekly or Monthly Reports

We will be providing you with professional, data-rich monthly reports. Each monthly report will be sent every 1st week of the month. As for the Weekly Report, we can generate them upon request but do take note that there will not be enough data in a week to make a comparative analysis. Thus, we do not recommend the weekly report setup - only on an as-needed basis.

ROI Analysis

The ROI analysis report, which is customized based on clients' goals for the PPC campaign, is also included in the Enterprise Level Monthly Reports we will be sending you.

Return on investment - or ROI - is the rate of revenues received for every dollar invested in an item or activity. In a marketing sense, knowing the ROI of your advertising and marketing campaigns helps you to identify which techniques are most effective for generating income for your business.

A/B Ad copy split-testing

With split testing, two or more ads are tested side by side to determine which performs better at a specific metric, allowing us to make improvements as necessary. Testing campaigns allows you to be aware of what works and what doesn't on your PPC campaign, making it a critical aspect of effective optimization.

http://www.searchmarketingstandard.com/maximizing-ppc-split-testing-strategies

Geo-targeting

Geo-targeting is an AdWords search campaign feature that allows advertisers to restrict ad distribution only to users with an IP address registered at an Internet Service Provider (ISP) with addresses assigned to a Designated Market Area (DMA), manually designated cities, or within a custom radius or polygonal range.

We will be setting the Geo-target of the campaign to ensure that the ads reach only your target market.

Ad scheduling

Ad scheduling lets you specify certain hours or days of the week when you want your AdWords ads to appear. For example, you might schedule your ads to run only on weekdays, or from 3:00 until 6:00 p.m. daily. With ad scheduling, a campaign can be programmed to run every day, or as seldom as 15 minutes per week.

Ad scheduling also includes an advanced setting which lets you adjust pricing for your ads during certain time periods. For example, if you find that your ads get the best results between 8:00 and 11:00 a.m., you can bid more for impressions or clicks during that period.
Ref: http://adwords.google.com/support/aw/bin/answer.py?hl=en&answer=117585

Adwords Campaign Experiments (ACE Test)
AdWords Campaign Experiments (ACE) is a tool that allows you to accurately test and measure changes to your keywords, bids, ad groups, ads, placements and more. ACE allows you to test and measure changes in real-time by executing your experimental campaign alongside your original campaign. By performing this type of simultaneous split test, we can tell you precisely the kind statistical changes your Search and Content campaign changes will produce.

Keyword Matching Options

We will be utilizing the four keyword matching options to help determine which Google searches can trigger your ads to appear. These four matching options can help control who sees your ads:

1. Broad match: keyword Allows your ad to show on similar phrases and relevant variations (The broad match modifier may also be used to further refine your broad keyword matches: +keyword.)

2. Phrase match: 'keyword' Allows your ad to show for searches that match the exact phrase.

3. Exact match: [keyword] Allows your ad to show for searches that match the exact phrase exclusively.

4. Negative match: -keyword Ensures your ad doesn't show for any search that includes that term

With some options, you'll enjoy more ad impressions, clicks, and conversions; with others, you'll get fewer impressions and more narrow targeting. By applying the appropriate matching options to your keywords, you can best meet your ROI goals.

http://adwords.google.com/support/aw/bin/answer.py?hl=en&answer=6100

Budget Management

Your daily budget is the amount that you're willing to spend on a specific AdWords campaign each day. AdWords displays your ads as often as possible while staying within your daily budget. When the budget limit is reached, your ads will typically stop showing for that day. How quickly your ads are shown during a given day is determined by your ad delivery setting.

Ref: http://adwords.google.com/support/aw/bin/answer.py?hl=en&answer=6312

Part of our AdWords campaign management is ensuring that you get the best ads placement possible with the budget you have allotted for your campaign.

Keyword Bid Management

A Keyword Bid is the dollar amount that an advertiser is willing to pay to display an ad relative to the competition. So in essence, Keyword Bid Management is how you control the bids to maximize the aforementioned dollar amount favorable to the advertiser.

Microsoft AdCenter

Microsoft Advertising adCenter is a tool to help you manage your search advertising campaign in Bing. Here, you only pay when someone clicks your ad.

Yahoo Search Marketing

This PPC platform is merged with Microsoft adCenter.

Facebook Ads

Advertising with Facebook Ads allows you to reach the exact audience you want with relevant targeted advertising.

AdWords Remarketing

Remarketing allows you to reach people who previously visited your website, and match the right people with the right message. You can show users these messages as they browse sites across the Google Display Network.

Pay Per Click Remarketing (Google AdWords)

Here are our Pay per Click Remarketing Packages designed to help your brand increase its visibility and recall among your target audience to help your business succeed further.

Hover over the question marks to get a quick description. You may also download this as a PDF with or without the extensive descriptions at the bottom part of this document.
In addition, you may view or download our primer on the marketing benefits of Pay per Click Remarketing for your business.

Monthly AdWords Budget Range
Represents the agreed upon, allotted monthly budget for the AdWords campaign.

Create Remarketing Tag Code
The remarketing tag is a small snippet of code that will be placed in all of the pages of your website. The remarketing code will help us define the page or pages in your website that will correspond to a remarketing list or lists that will be the target audience of the remarketing campaign.

Install Remarketing Tag Code

We will install the remarketing tag across your website. The remarketing tag works for visitors who come to your website using any device. It may be a desktop computer, a laptop computer, or a mobile device. There is no need to create a separate tag or list for mobile visitors.

Set the pages that will be triggers to retarget users

The pages of your website will be defined as to which ones will trigger remarketing to retarget its visitors through ads across the Google Display Network.

Set the pages that will be hidden on retargeting

The pages of your website that will not be set to trigger remarketing will also be defined.

Create Remarketing List(s)

A remarketing list is a collection of cookies from people who visited a website. This is the list you'd target your ads to that is based on the defined pages that they visited. Creating the list is one of the most important steps in setting up a remarketing campaign.

Create Membership Duration

When you create a remarketing list, you can decide how long a visitor's cookie stays on your list. We recommend setting a duration related to the length of time you expect your ad to be relevant for the visitor. In general, you should align the membership duration with the length of your sales cycle.

Create Remarketing Banner Text (for approval)

Remarketing banner ads will be created to reflect your branding and key messages to effect brand recall to maximize impressions and/or with a call to action to influence high click through rates.

Align Banner Ads to Landing Page

Your banner ads will be aligned to your existing landing pages for high coherence and relevancy to promote higher conversion rates.

Set the number of times the ad copy will appear daily

We can set a cap on remarketing banner ad impressions on a daily basis to make sure that your remarketing audience will not be too much bombarded with your banners ads.

Traffic Estimation to determine PPC search recommendation

A remarketing list must have at least 100 cookies on it before you can show an ad on the Display Network to people on the list. For websites with fewer than 100 cookies, a PPC search campaign is recommended to boost traffic.

Setup Remarketing Cancellation Triggers

Cancellation can be set by defining a particular page or pages that when visited by an audience in a list-that audience will no longer be shown remarketing banner ads.

Testing of Banner Ads

With split testing, two or more ads are tested side by side to determine which performs better at a specific metric, allowing us to make improvements as necessary. Testing banner ads allows you to be aware of what works and what doesn't on your PPC campaign, making it a critical aspect of effective optimization.

Testing of Landing Pages

Testing landing pages allows you to be aware of what works, what converts visitors to customers at a higher rate and what doesn't on your PPC campaign, making it a critical aspect of effective optimization.

Display Network Optimization

We optimize to appear in the most targeted and high-traffic websites in the display network where your target audience go to.

Budget Management

Your daily budget is the amount that you're willing to spend on a specific AdWords campaign each day. AdWords displays your ads as often as possible while staying within your daily budget. When the budget limit is reached, your ads will typically stop showing for that day. How quickly your ads are shown during a given day is determined by your ad delivery setting.

Impression Capping Optimization

We will manage your campaign towards determining the optimal number of impressions that convert based on your budget. Very few impressions produce little impact while too many impressions may also backfire. Impression capping optimization means finding the right balance.

Delay Targeting

With a list targeting rules, remarketing to your audience only after a given period is doable thereby aligning your remarketing ads with the time that your audience (for example) due to renew their membership.

Target Existing Customers

With list targeting rule, you may target existing customers visiting your website with remarketing banner ads with messaging aimed at retaining them.

Online Reputation Management

Potential customers change purchase decisions when they see bad reviews, posts and comments online which can spread in various channels such as in search engine results and in social media channels. In today's world of highly connected and engaged customers, any negative commentary (malicious or not) about your products and services can wreak havoc to your bottom line. You cannot afford not to do ORM!

Number of Keywords

This consists of a group of words that, when typed in the search engine results pages, lists web pages that have negative or bad press about the individual/company. The agreed upon target key phrase is what we will be using when optimizing the profiles or web pages we create to push down the unwanted or negative pages.

Primary Web Reputation Analysis

The initial analysis for Online Reputation Management (ORM) involves collecting information on the popularity, current standing and online reputation of your website. The data we have gathered at this stage will be our benchmark for the reputation management campaign before the ORM is performed, allowing us to track our progress and address any negative publicity.

ORM Keyword Research

Upon generating the list of keywords associated with negative or unwanted web pages, the most ideal keywords to target for a particular site will be selected from the list. The selection of ideal keywords depends on several factors, including the competition for a particular keyword and their relevance to your business.

Web 2.0 Blog Setups

Through social media platforms, a Web 2.0 site allows users to collaborate as creators or as prosumers (producer-consumers) of user-generated content in a virtual community. This is in stark contrast to websites, where users (consumers) are limited to the passive viewing of content that was created for them.

We will be setting up and optimizing Web 2.0 Blogs representing your company's website.

Blog Link-Wheel Setup

A link wheel is one of the fastest methods of getting quality backlinks to your site from authority sites.

In theory, a link wheel consists of separate URLs with content and two anchor text links placed within said content. One of the links refers to the site you are trying to rank. The other link will take users to another URL within the wheel. This particular URL will also have content on it that contains two links: one that sends users to your main site (called the 'money site') and the other to yet another URL within the wheel. This creates a virtual wheel with your main site in the middle and other URLs around it, creating a web of interconnected websites.

After setting up Web 2.0 blogs on the same topic as your main blog or website, we will then write unique, quality articles on each of these mini sites. We will add a link to your main website or blog and another link to one of the other blogs we created to establish the link wheel.

Press Release Writing and Keyword Optimization

ORM press releases feature important updates in your life/company. The primary purpose is to populate the Web with positive content related to you or the company. ORM press releases rank incredibly well in search engines because they are sources of fresh content about you or the company.

Our press releases follow proper keyword optimization. We normally target one to two keywords in each article while maintaining the recommended keyword density. Our method of inserting keywords involves meeting SEO requirements and, at the same time, ensuring that the keywords appear organic in the content.

The syndication of these press releases provides essential, strong backlinks to our target pages via keyword anchor text. Each press release is strategically linked back to the corresponding pages of the website.

Article Writing and Keyword Optimization

ORM articles are an essential component of an ORM campaign. They are written about the keyword subjects and are not directly associated with you or the company, unless you or the company name is chosen as a target keyword. Their primary purpose is to populate the Web with positive content related to you or the company.

Our articles follow proper keyword optimization. We normally target one to two keywords in each article while maintaining the recommended keyword density. Our method of inserting keywords involves meeting SEO requirements and, at the same time, ensuring that the keywords appear organic in the content.

The distribution of articles that are optimized with relevant keywords and contain an embedded link pointing back to the target website will help build a strong linking structure.

Blog Article Writing and Keyword Optimization

ORM blog posts feature topics of interest about you or the company. These blog posts act as another web page, complete with an optimized URL and H1 tags. Their primary purpose is to populate the Web with positive content related to you or the company.

Our blog posts follow proper keyword optimization. We normally target one to two keywords in each article while maintaining the recommended keyword density. Our method of inserting keywords involves meeting SEO requirements and, at the same time, ensuring that the keywords appear organic in the content.

The addition of these blog posts to the site expands the site's overall size while providing useful information to its target audience.

Review Publication

Upon being furnished with reviews you have collected, we will publish each of them to one of the major review publication websites.

Pages Indexing Analysis - Google & Bing

Indexed Pages are the pages on a website that have been indexed or found by search engines, like Google. It is very important that the majority, if not all of your website's pages, are indexed in the search engines. Otherwise, users will not be able to find or access them.

Using a special search query format, we will be checking Google and Bing for the indexing status of the target site. The results will help determine if the site is being crawled by the major search engines, how many pages are being crawled, and which version of URLs (WWW or non-WWW) are to be followed for optimization.

Indexing refers to how many of your website pages the search engines look at. The more pages indexed, the better. We analyze indexed page counts to see which pages of your site aren't being indexed and why. We then use this information to determine the best course of action.

Site Authority Analysis - MozRank, Domain Authority

These scores are measures of your sites' Authority in the eyes of search engines. The more Authority you have, the higher up the search results you appear.

What does this mean for your business? Are your scores higher or lower than your competitors? A higher score is favorable. As you improve your SEO, your Authority scores will increase as a direct result.

Backlink Count and Referring Domains Overview

We will be generating a report with the total backlinks and referring domains count.

Integrative Link Placement Research

One-way links are links to your site from sites that do not receive a link from your site in return. They send a powerful message to the search engines that your website is so valuable or interesting or useful that other sites want to tell people about it.

Prior to every one way link placement, we thoroughly research blog or forum opportunities relating to our target website and keywords. A manual search for blog related posts or forums is performed and then thoroughly analyzed as a link building solution. There are a number of different factors that we take into consideration throughout the process.

These include, but are not limited to, the following:

1. Niche/Keyword Relation
2. Recent posts no older than 6 months
3. Non-pornographic posts and/or sites
4. Non-competition sites allowed
5. Non-spammy sites allowed

Competitive Link Finder

We will be finding links your competition has that you don't and then show you where they are getting them from. Using this information, we can then decide whether or not we would like to go after the same links. The links will include lots of link juice information about the quality of the page it's coming from, the PageRank, etc.

Vipassana Meditation

This is off topic but I feel very strongly that a human being must have balance in Health, Spirit and Business.

The technique of Vipassana Meditation is a simple, practical way to achieve real peace of mind and lead a happy, useful life.

Vipassana means "to see things as they really are" and is a logical process of mental purification through self-observation.

From time to time, we all experience agitation, frustration and disharmony. When we suffer, we do not keep our misery limited to ourselves; instead, we keep distributing it to others.

Certainly this is not a proper way to live.

We all long to live at peace within ourselves, and with those around us. After all, human beings are social beings; we have to live and interact with others. How, then, can we live peacefully? How can we remain harmonious ourselves, and maintain peace and harmony around us?

Vipassana enables us to experience peace and harmony: it purifies the mind, freeing it from suffering and deep-seated causes of suffering. The practice leads step-by-step to the highest spiritual goal of full liberation from all mental defilements.

To learn Vipassana meditation it is necessary to take a ten-day residential course under the guidance of a qualified teacher. Ten days of sustained practice have been found to be the minimum amount of time in which the essentials of the technique can be learned so that Vipassana can be applied in daily life.
As of this writing, I have been to 13 of these courses in the last 15 years. If this is of interest to you, the course is free, lodging is free and meals are free. All run on donation from students that get value.

www.Dhamma.org

www.ingramcontent.com/pod-product-compliance
Lightning Source LLC
Chambersburg PA
CBHW051853170526
45168CB00001B/92